ACCEPTANCE
OF WHAT IS

Also by
Wayne (Ram Tzu) Liquorman:

NO WAY for the Spiritually "Advanced"

ACCEPTANCE OF WHAT IS

A BOOK ABOUT NOTHING

BY

WAYNE LIQUORMAN

EDITED BY
CATHERINE ASCHE

Advaita Press

Published in the USA by

Advaita Press
PO Box 3479
Redondo Beach, CA 90277
Tel: 310-376-9636
Email: fellowship@advaita.org
www.advaita.org

Cover Design : Chetna Bhatt

Cover Photo: Robert (aka Richard) Daly

ISBN: 0-929448-19-7 (soft cover)
0-929448-20-0 (hard cover)
Library of Congress Card Number: 99-066782

CONTENTS

EDITOR'S NOTE

When, over lunch at a Mexican food restaurant a short walk from his house, Wayne asked me to write an editor's note for this book, which was, by then, at the proofreading stage, my immediate response was, "Oh no, do I have to? Everything changes every five minutes, so whatever I might write today, if I looked at it tomorrow, I'd think it was awful." Wayne was gently insistent, suggesting I put pen to paper and, "Just see what happens." This is what happened.

In early February, 1999, a group of us, including Wayne, were in the chatroom at the Advaita Fellowship website (http://www.advaita.org).

Here is an excerpt from that conversation.
(Wayne is <. > and the editor is <cat>).

<.> robert adams once suggested we throw a jnani convention and anyone who showed up would be immediately disqualified
<cat> hehehehehe
<cat> excellent
<bala> who is robert adams?
<.> ramana devotee, who taught in sedona
<.> died last year
<.> quite a character
<bala> did you meet him?
<bala> ah and his picture was on the wall where you lectured in sedona?
<.> yes bala
<bala> i heard it on the tapes
<cat> did he write books?

<.> no, but there was a very nice book done by a devotee, our hostess in Santa Fe
<.> ananda devi
<bala> what's it called?
<.> silence of the heart
<bala> aha thanks
<cat> and when can we expect another book from you?
<.> as soon as you edit one
<cat> ahh ok
<cat> hehehe
<cat> gladly
<.> best get started soon, both ramesh and dorothy are on my ass about it.

I really did not take this seriously until, that same day, Wayne emailed me a large number of transcriptions of his recorded talks and told me to see what I could do with them. Having no editing experience whatsoever, I was hesitant and eager to be told how to proceed. To my frustration at the time, but later gratitude,Wayne refused to give instruction, simply advising me to, "Let it flow." I emailed Blayne Bardo in Bombay for some tips. He was, at the time, editing Ramesh's book, *Your Head in the Tiger's Mouth,* and he was very generous with practical advice of a technical nature. But the scope and structure of the book seemed to be left to me to work out, and I wondered whether I was up to the task.

One morning when I woke up, all at once there appeared a clear idea of the book's structure and of how to proceed. By sacrificing some of the authentic flow of the live talks which can often leap about from one topic to another according to the needs of those present, (and are in any case available on audio and videotape) the questions and answers could be grouped according to topic, thus giving a full focus to each. This, it was hoped, would present Wayne's teachings clearly and accessibly to both newcomer and 'advanced seeker.' The plan was to read through hard copies of all the material, making notes in the margins regarding what the discussion was about. From these notes I would compile a huge list of subtopics and then see if these could be condensed into 6 or 7 major topics. These would become the chapters. This method proved delightfully successful.

Seven major topics emerged, and then it was simply a matter of taking scissors to paper and sorting into folders, and then taking each topic folder one by one and constructing chapters. The joy and ease with which all this was accomplished gave me some cause for concern. Our conditioning often tells us that anything worthwhile must be accomplished with great difficulty. Something that is done with pure enjoyment can hardly be any good. You'll have to judge this for yourself, but I am truly astounded that a book happened at all, let alone one which could pass Wayne's scrutiny!

It was only after all the chapters had been constructed that I noticed that in the structure of the book there was a movement matching my own 'quest,' from Jnana to Bhakti (the intellectual to the devotional). This, I believe, was also the direction that Wayne's 'path' had taken. After an introductory disclaimer, we leap straight into a chapter on the "Teachings," full of talk of Noumenon and phenomena, Consciousness, time and the new physics.

Lest this be offputting, readers such as those with a more devotional orientation should feel free to skip over this, or even start at the back of the book and work the other way. Following the exposition of the Advaitic Teachings, there is a chapter on how the seeking begins, followed by a whole chapter on the sense of personal doership. This latter seemed necessary, as it was by far the most discussed topic in the various recorded talks. The chapter called Paths discusses the various means and

methods by which the aspirant seeks to attain enlightenment and why these are exercises in futility. The following
chapter, Enlightenment, discusses what enlightenment is
and isn't. Finally, the chapter, Guru and Disciple speaks
of the mysterious 'Resonance' that happens between sage
and disciple through which the Guru manifests.

    I hope the reader finds as much enjoyment in explor-
ing this book as I had in putting it together.

Catherine Asche
Hermosa Beach, CA
September 1999

♋   ♋   ♋

ACKNOWLEDGEMENTS

Many people contributed to the making of this book. The editor would like to heartily thank the following people:

Transcribers: Jane Adams, Mandie Bava, Dyan Ellebracht, Todd Haydon, Sajjana and Katrina Small.

Proofreaders: Anton Asche, Christopher Bava, Mandie Bava, Alex Brown, Susan Cooney, Dorothy Doyle, Todd Haydon, Daniel Heller, Steven Hoel, Peter Marjason, John Montgomery, JoAnne Franz-Moore, Shannon Nibley, Jeffrey Padawer, Steven Rudder, Mallory Shimada, Heiner Siegelmann, Roy Strassman and Donna Tonery.

Editing advice: Blayne Bardo.

Layout and design: James Corless.

Illustration: Ted Kingdon.

Support and encouragement: my family and friends, especially my daughter Amanda Grey, my partner Michael Andrews, my brother Thomas Asche and all the wonderful people from the Advaita Fellowship Chatroom.

♋   ♋   ♋

For my beloved Ramesh:

Who was
First a window
Then a door

Just Sit There

Just sit there right now
Don't do a thing. Just rest.

For your separation from God
Is the hardest work in the world.

Let me bring you trays of food
And something
That you like to drink.

You can use my words
As a cushion
For your head.

Hafiz

♋

I'll play it first and tell you what it is later.
Miles Davis

♋︎   ♋︎   ♋︎

Truth disappears in the telling of it.
Lawrence Durrell

♋︎   ♋︎   ♋︎

We start, then, with nothing, pure zero. But this is not
the nothing of negation. For not means other than, and
other is merely a synonym of the ordinal numeral
second. As such it implies a first; while the present pure
zero is prior to every first. The nothing of negation is
the nothing of death, which comes second to, or after,
everything. But this pure zero is the nothing of not
having been born. There is no individual thing, no
compulsion, outward nor inward, no law. It is the
germinal nothing, in which the whole universe is
involved or foreshadowed. As such, it is absolutely
undefined and unlimited possibility—boundless
possibility. There is no compulsion and no law. It is
boundless freedom.

Charles S. Peirce, *Logic of Events* (1898)

♋︎   ♋︎   ♋︎

Ram Tzu knows this...

Silence may be the purest medium
For the transmission of truth.
But it makes for
Damned short books
And awful dinner parties.

ONE

BUYER BEWARE

TRUTH DISAPPEARS
IN THE TELLING OF IT

For those of you who are hearing me for the first time I want to emphasize that nothing I say is the Truth. I make *no claims whatsoever* that one word coming out of my mouth is the Truth.

Now I am not unique in this. None of the teachers that you've either read or heard are speaking the Truth. Truth can't be spoken. All of these words, all of these concepts are simply pointers, indicators of a Truth that is right here—that is ever-present—as clear, and as unmasked as it could possibly be.

Ramana Maharshi used the image of a concept as being like a thorn that is used to remove some other thorn that is, let's say, embedded in your foot. So you have a thorn (which is some concept about how things are) and it's embedded in you. The sage comes and uses another concept in the hopes of removing that embedded concept with this second concept. If the embedded concept is removed both concepts become superfluous—they get discarded. The thorn that's being utilized to remove the other thorn has no *intrinsic* value. After it has done its job you don't wax rhapsodic over what a great thorn it was. Its value is only as a tool.

Ramana Maharshi's big thorn was: Ask yourself, "Who Am I?"...Ask yourself, "Who's asking the question?"...Ask yourself, "Who wants to know?" That was his 'thorn of choice,' if you will. In the hands of this Master, in a specific moment, in a specific application when he would identify intuitively what the seeker coming to him needed, he would utilize this concept.

Later, some of the people sitting around watching him and listening to him would say, "Remember that fellow who came and asked a question and Bhagwan said, "Who wants to know?" And when Bhagwan said that, you could see in the face of that fellow that it cut right to the quick of the matter...that in that instant he *saw!* What a magical, wondrous, fantastic tool this is!"

So they go away, and one day they overhear someone complaining about the confusion that arises in the seeking. And they say, "You're confused? So *who* is confused? *(laughter) Who* thinks that they're confused? Huh? Huh? Huh?" *(laughter)* And chances are very good that if you have been wandering around in spiritual circles of late, you've run into lots of people with knowing smirks on their faces who are asking, "So who wants to know? Who's asking the question, huh?" As if this is some kind of magic incantation. *(laughter)* And of course it isn't. It's just another tool, another concept.

It's as if you were watching a brain surgeon...you sit in the operating theatre and you watch him take his scalpel and make an incision. And he makes another incision, and cuts through the cranium and the brain is exposed. He takes the scalpel and makes another tiny little incision over here, and he sews the patient back up again. And amazingly, the patient is healed! It's fantastic! So...you watch again. You peer down into the operating theatre, and you see him cut through there, and make a little incision there...then he puts the scalpel down, and goes off. You sneak down and you steal the scalpel. *(laughter)* Now *you* have the scalpel. You can now go and do brain surgery! You have the healing instrument. And one day you run across somebody who has the exact symptoms as this guy who was just on the operating table, and you say, "I can help you out, lie down!" You apply this tool, this magic scalpel, in approximately the same place that you saw the surgeon apply it...and there's a good chance you're going to make a bloody mess. Because this is a tool. All of these concepts, every single one of these concepts is simply a tool. And as long as you can remember the fact that these are merely tools, merely pointers, you'll save yourself a lot of trouble.

Generally, by the time you've gotten here you've read a lot, you've been to a lot of teachers, you have absorbed a vast number of concepts, and many of them are contradictory. How do you reconcile what this teacher said with what that teacher said? I mean, you've sat with this teacher; you know that this person is a genuine teacher. There's no question of him scamming you. And yet he's saying something that is utterly and completely different from what this one over here is saying. How do you reconcile these? The way you reconcile them is to understand that neither of them is true. So it isn't a matter of choosing which one is true, it's just recognizing that neither are true. From that standpoint it makes it a lot easier. Those concepts are applicable only in the moment. And their real usefulness is revealed when they are in the hands of the sage.

♋   ♋   ♋

There are no whole truths. All truths are half truths. It is trying to treat them as whole truths that plays the devil.

Alfred North Whitehead

♋   ♋   ♋

You like your truth
Abstract enough
To be palatable.
Rawness sticks in your throat.
You prefer the soaring poetry of
What is coming
To the pedestrian presence
Of what's here now.

Ram Tzu

♋   ♋   ♋

"If fifty million people say a foolish thing, it is still a foolish thing."

Anatole France

♋   ♋   ♋

Ultimately
All attempts at discussing Truth
Leave you sounding like a fortune cookie.

Ram Tzu

♋   ♋   ♋

The great enemy of the truth is very often not the lie—deliberate, contrived, and dishonest—but the myth—persistent, persuasive, and unrealistic.

John Fitzgerald Kennedy

TWO

EACHINGS

THE BASICS

All there is, is Consciousness.
Consciousness is all there is.

The rest of this book is just variations on that theme. Though even *that* is only a pointer. *That* is not the Truth. The Truth can not be spoken. That is a concept...a fairly elegant one as concepts go, but a concept nonetheless.

This Truth that is being pointed at, is a truth that is beyond the capacity of the mind to understand; because the mind is a divisive tool. The mind's job is to compare or, as Ram Tzu would say:

First...

You use your mind as
The ultimate jigsaw.
You take Totality
And cut it up
Into a million tiny pieces.

Then...
Having tired of that game,
You sit down, and try to
Reassemble this jumble of pieces
Into something comprehensible.

Ram Tzu knows...

God invented time
Just so you could do this.

That is the game of the mind. And though the mind is not suited to the job of understanding Truth, it is the mind that is employed by the seeker on this path of *jnana* or knowledge. The mind is set to the task of finding out what it is. That is a task tantamount to standing in your own boots and lifting yourself by your bootstraps.

And the teachers exhort you to lift harder! You must be more earnest in your lifting! Lift! Lift! Lift!

This path of *jnana*, this path of knowledge, requires a transcendence of the mind; and that can only happen when the mind is utterly, thoroughly, *completely* exhausted. After you have sought every *possible* avenue into which you might inquire and *know*, after you have thought again and again that you've GOT IT, only to find it slip through your fingers like jello; only then can there possibly be some kind of surrender, some kind of *acceptance* of the fact that the mind will not get you there. And it isn't enough to just pay lip service to the fact of, "The mind isn't gonna help; the mind isn't gonna know it"—That is something the mind KNOWS! *(Loud laughter)* That's the *new* truth that you're holding sacred!

It gets subtler and subtler. That which you think you *know*, gets subtler and subtler. It's really a process very much like a dog chasing its tail. Your mind is set in motion seeking itself, chasing itself, trying to catch itself. And if you have a mind that is strong, that has a lot of intellect behind it, you can get spinning VERY fast! And you can *catch up!* You can *(laughter) gain*, on yourself! And the faster you get spinning, the closer that you gain on yourself and perhaps, if there is Grace, you will disappear up your own ass!

And this describes the path of *jnana*. I don't know what *veda* or *sutra* it is in, but that is essentially what we've set out to do: to inquire deeply, to look at that which is asking the questions; to look at that which is seeking; and to find out: is there any substance there? And it's not something that I can do for you. I can sit up here all day and talk about it, and if you trust me...which is dicey to begin with...then you'll say, "He's telling the truth, what he's saying is valid, I believe him."

But I am NOT telling the truth. What I am saying here is NOT the truth. At the very best, these are pointers towards that truth, towards That which Is, That which is the Source and the Substance of everything; that Consciousness which is *all there is*. That which is our True Nature, That which we *Are*.

♋   ♋   ♋

THE NOTHING OF ADVAITA

This teaching is incredibly, incredibly simple. There's nothing to it — literally, NOTHING to it. Of course the "nothing" that we're talking about is the nothing of the Sufi *fakir*, who wanders into the highest court in the land. He plops down in the King's throne, and the chief Minister walks up to him and he says, "What are you doing sitting there, do you think that you're a Minister of this Court?" And the Sufi says, "Nah, I'm not just a Minister of this Court, I'm more than that." The Chief Minister says, "Well, you're certainly not the Chief Minister, I'm the Chief Minister!" The Sufi says, "No, I'm not the Chief Minister, I'm more than that." "What! Do you think you're the King? You're sitting on the King's throne!"

The Sufi says, "No, not the King. I'm more than the King." "MORE than the King, do you think you're the Emperor?" The Sufi says, "Nah, I don't think I'm the Emperor, I'm much more than the Emperor." "More than the Emperor, do you think you're GOD?" The Sufi says, "Nah! I don't think I'm God, I'm more than that." The Chief Minister was aghast. "More than God, there's NOTHING!!" The Sufi says, "Precisely! I am that NOTH-ING!"

That's the Nothing we're talking about. This was always one of my favorite stories from Ramesh. He told it all the time. And then one day somebody came in with a corollary story, which goes with it well. I see it all the time, as I travel around meeting "spiritual people." The story is about a Rabbi who goes into the Sanctuary, opens the Ark, and sees the Torah sitting there. He's overcome with the incredible beauty of it. So with emotion, and with piety, he falls to his knees, looks up to heaven and says, "God, I'M NOTHING! I am *NOTHING* !"

The second rabbi, the assistant rabbi comes walking by the Sanctuary and sees the Chief Rabbi on his knees in front of the Ark, and he's so astonished, and astound-ed, and impressed by this display of piety, that he too rushes up, falls to his knees next to the Chief Rabbi and says "God, *I* am Nothing!! I AM *Nothing* !!"

Now I don't know how many Jews we've got here, but certainly on this Saturday morning, not any ortho-dox ones...*(loud laughter)* Always in the Temple they have an employee who is not a Jew, to do things around the Temple on the Sabbath. So this fellow is walking by the Sanctuary, and he sees the two rabbis in front of the Ark, and he's so taken with their show of piety, that *he* rushes down, and *he* falls to his knees next to the two rabbis, and he shouts: "GOD, *I* am Nothing! *I AM NOTHING* ! " And the first rabbi nudges the second rabbi and says, "So look who thinks he's Nothing!" *(laughter)*

We see this in Advaitic circles all the time, *(piously)* "I don't exist." "None of this is real." "What I truly am is Consciousness." Delivered with just the right amount of conviction. The unreality, the insubstantiality of this manifestation, which is so often pointed to by various teachers and sages, *is a pointer*. All of this is as real as you are—to paraphrase Ramana Maharshi. I think he was asked, "Are all the gods and spirits real?," and his response was, "They are as real as you are."

This manifestation, this phenomenal manifestation, *is* an aspect of the Totality. It is not some kind of tragic mistake that you created in your ignorance. This entire, incredibly rich, magnificent, beautiful, horrible, wonderful, manifestation, *all of it* is an aspect of God, an aspect of the Total. And it is unreal to the extent that it has *no independent existence*. It does not exist independently of this animating Consciousness, but rather, is an aspect of it.

Anybody have a Kleenex—preferably an unused one? Thank you.

I will now materialize…*(rolling Kleenex tissue into a ball between palms and holding it up between finger and thumb)* This is Consciousness—the Source and the Substance of everything. This is *everything*, everything that ever was, ever will be…Consciousness at rest, Consciousness not manifest, Consciousness without feature…no thing…No-thing-ness…Noumenon.

It is infinite potentiality, not yet expressed into any thing; thus, it is no thing. Because it is infinite potentiality and not an empty, nihilistic void, but is rather, infinite potential, it *must*, as part of its nature, activise, actualize. And whether you call that Genesis or the Big Bang, doesn't matter; this *(pulls out a large tendril from Kleenex ball without detaching it)* is the point at which that which is infinite potential expresses into manifestation, into phenomenality, into *all this stuff of life*. Every bit of it! And it all arises at once. So out of this incredible potentiality extrudes Universes *(pulls out 'galactic' extrusions of tissue)* and Solar Systems, and out of the Solar System is extruded, *(twirls out tendrils from that already extruded)* this planetary system, and this little planetary system here is extruding out into Earth, and out of this Earth are extruding all of these various body-mind mechanisms. And they arise and they live a little span and then they fall back *(compresses tendrils back into ball)* into this infinite potentiality; and new ones are created *(pulls out tendril from other side of the ball)* extruded out of this...so that you have this one particular extrusion *(pulls out long "tower" upstanding from ball)*—we'll call it 'you'—which is simply an aspect of this entire phenomenal manifestation.

One of the curious things about this aspect, this particular extrusion, is that it is given a sense of separateness, a sense of personal doership, in which it feels that it is in some way separated, from That. But THIS is Oneness. This is the sum total of everything. There is no 'this.' *(tears extrusion off and holds it away in the air)* There is only *This* (the Total) expressing, extruding out into an infinite number of extrusions, many of which consider themselves separate, having the 'hypnosis,' if you will, of separateness; but there *is* no separateness. Everything is connected; everything is this Oneness. There is no twoness. There is only the *experience* of twoness; there is only the *appearance* of twoness; because the connectedness isn't experienced, isn't seen, isn't felt. But that doesn't change the fundamental nature of things. The fundamental nature of things is that all there is, is Consciousness, Consciousness is all there is. And when this particular *(Kleenex tendril)* body-mind mechanism has finished its appointed span, it's de-extruded; and you say, "What happens to it?" That's the basic question everyone wants to know—what's going to happen to ME when I am no longer extruded? *(Loud laughter)*

Well, you were never separate. You were never anything but This. *(Kleenex ball)* Therefore, nothing happens to you. That which you consider yourself to be *(extrusion)* becomes that *(ball)*—all of the thoughts and the memories and the experiences that happened through that extrusion, don't go anywhere. They are still part of the whole. Everything continues to be part of the whole. New body-mind mechanisms may be extruded over here—*(pulls out Kleenex from other quarter of the ball)* and some of the memories from there may well show up, here. And if this particular extrusion has a sense of personal doership, has a sense of self, it's going to say, "These are MY memories. *I* lived five hundred years ago! *(laughter)* That was *my* life!"

All there is, is Consciousness. Consciousness is all there is. But for this dance, this *lila* to go on, for this play, this dream, to happen, the sense of personal doership is integral. It arises at around the age of two-and-a-half, or so; the baby goes from experiencing being an instrument—a direct experience—to one which begins to say "I". "I want. *I'm* doing. Give ME." Before that, it's, "Bobby wants, Jane wants." At around two-and-a-half, it becomes "*I* want." In most body-mind mechanisms, that sense of 'me,' that sense of 'me' as a separate point of doership continues right up until death. In a few cases, at some point, that firmly held belief comes into question. Something happens in the life of that body-mind mechanism that calls into question this fundamental concept that, "I'm the doer."

And that's the point at which you become a seeker. That's the point at which your life takes an inexorable turn, that brings you into places like this, talking about bizarre stuff like this. The seeking begins. And the seeking leads you. And through the course of the seeking come insights, come experiences in which you *know* at the most fundamental level that you're not the doer. You experience the *impersonality* of the Universe, the Unity, the underlying Unity.

That keeps you going. And that which is seeking is nothing other than that which is sought.

♋   ♋   ♋

WHAT IS CONSCIOUSNESS?

Consciousness is a term that I have a lot of difficulty with and always have. I see it as awareness but it still doesn't feel right. It is elusive.

Elusive it is indeed!

I don't know how to express it, but I guess I think of it as awareness in the larger sense of the term.

The term, Consciousness, is often used in this teaching with a capital 'C' to indicate that Consciousness is synonymous with such terms as God, Source, Totality, Oneness, Unity, Tao, etc.. It is that which is the source and the substance of everything that is physical, of everything that is phenomenal as part of this manifestation. It had to come from somewhere and just as a spider creates a web out of itself, Consciousness has spun this phenomenal manifestation out of itself. Now, the point at which that particular analogy breaks down is that the web is at no time, at no point, independent of Consciousness. The manifestation; all of this, all of us, everything, is in no way disconnected from that original source. So it is both the animus as well as the *corpus*, the substance and that which animates it!

Okay. My problem is, then what is behind that?

Sure. That is an absolutely legitimate question. Because when we objectify Consciousness as some *thing* the next logical step is, "Okay what field does that thing exist in?" but we are constrained by language, and language by its structure is in subject-object relationship. Every sentence has a subject and an object. Whenever we think about something, whenever we utter the first word about something we have objectified it. When Lao Tzu wrote the Tao Te Ching, the first line he wrote was, "The Tao that can be named is not the true Tao." As soon as you talk about it, as soon as you have a mental concept (you don't have to articulate it) as soon as the image forms in mind, then that has become objectified. So the moment we start to speak about it, it isn't It. So all of these concepts are not It. They are simply pointers, hopefully in the general direction of It. The touchstone phrase is: "All there is is Consciousness." But even that is not completely It.

℆   ℆   ℆

WHO IS THE SEEKER?

If the Self is already enlightened, who is the seeker?

The seeker is the sought.

Isn't that also the Self?

All there is is the Self. And that is the crux of the Divine paradox, that there is this sense of separateness that is in fact *not* separateness. The mere fact that you misperceive something does not change its nature. An example is that you walk in and you see a snake on the ground, and you react. You jump back. You're afraid. The adrenaline rushes through your body. All the reactions take place that are appropriate to a snake being there. But on closer examination the snake is revealed to be a rope. Now, your misperception, your belief that that was a snake made you act in certain ways. But it was never a snake. It was always a rope.

So who has that belief?

That belief is a function of mind.

So mind is out to destroy itself and to preserve itself?

The mind of a seeker is out to destroy itself…in theory. *(laughter)* When it comes right down to crunch time, mind will never destroy itself.

And it doesn't exist anyhow?

It does not exist in "reality," whatever that is. It has no *independent* existence. It is literally as real as you are.

That's not much to brag about.

But there is clearly a *sense* of reality to it. The appearance of the snake seems very real, even though it's an appearance. Even though it has no substance. Your subjective experience of it is that it might as well be real, from your perspective, in that moment. You will respond according to that belief, until such time as the snake is revealed to be a rope.

☺   ☺   ☺

ILLUSION

Many teachers in the books I have studied say that nothing is here, that it's all an illusion.

So if "Nothing is here" who is writing and reading all these books? *(laughter)*

I guess the appearance that likes the idea that, "Nothing is here." (laughter) There is a big gap in there that nobody knows how to explain.

Yes, this notion of nothing being here is kind of an interesting one. It is talked about quite a bit in these so-called "spiritual circles," that it is all just a dream. And as notions go, that one is a pretty interesting one. In the case of all of these concepts, the opportunity for misunderstanding the intent of the concept is quite great, and this notion that nothing exists flies in the face of all of our experience. I'm always interested in the question: To whom does this occur that nothing exists? What is the nature of that which knows or speculates that things don't exist. Does *it* exist? What was pointed out to me by Ramesh fairly early on was that the only thing that none of us could really argue is that there is existence— that I exist. Now what the nature of that "I" is that is saying that, that is experiencing that, that feels that, is open to a lot of argument. But the underlying experience, the underlying knowing, the underlying presence is that there is something here. There is something here! There is existence here. When you clear away all the bullshit, all the conceptual framework, everything, and you move it all aside, what is left inarguably is that there is something there! And that is the only Truth. By Truth I mean that which can brook no argument. And that point of existence is what is referred to as the "I Am." This "I Am,"—before there is an "I am Mark" or "I am Bill"—this "I Am" exists prior to the development or recognition of someone—someone individuated. Prior to that, there is a sense of presence and that sense of presence is the contact point, if you will. It is where the Noumenal meets the phenomenal. And I say that it is a notional contact point because the Noumenal and the phenomenal are not separate. So they never meet anywhere because they are never separate; but it is a notional point because we as identified observers exist in subject-object relationship.

What is 'Noumenal'? I've never heard it before.

The Noumenon is That from which phenomena springs. It's synonymous with God, Consciousness, Tao, Totality, Source. It is the undifferentiated 'state' of Oneness. I also had never heard that term prior to meeting Ramesh, and *he* apparently got it from Wei Wu Wei. It's certainly not a term that's in common usage.

♋   ♋   ♋

THE DREAM ANALOGY

Perhaps you could tell me a little more about the concept of the dream. It seems to me that what Ramesh is saying is that all of this is a dream—this gathering in this room is a dream, and yet there are distinctions between what happens in my waking state and the dream state. For ex-

ample, I made a decision to be here today, and here I am. But I don't think I have anything to do with what happens in my dream state. So I make a distinction there. Can one make such a distinction, or is a distinction being made, or is it all just one big dream functioning at different times of the day?

Well, the dream analogy is just that—an analogy. Ramesh is not saying that this world is literally a dream. What he is saying is that it is *like* your 'personal' dream at night inasmuch as it has no independent substance independent of the dreamer. Now in this case, the dreamer is Consciousness. You can say that this universe that we inhabit is the dream of Consciousness, that all of this is an appearance in Consciousness. For example, in your dream at night there are mountains, and if there is a geologist in your dream, that geologist will have dream tools with which he will measure the dream mountain and come up with findings that that mountain is 800 million years old. So within the context of the dream, there's a mountain that's been measured to be 800 million years old, and you've only been dreaming for half an hour! How can there be a mountain that's 800 million years old?! Within the context of your dream there is no problem. So within the context of this living dream, there is Mt. Everest that is millions of years old. There are all of these characters who interact with one another, who have relationships with one another. They move about within the dream. But the ultimate understanding is that they have no independent existence.

Would you say that this manifestation is basically like a dog and pony show?

It is God's dog and pony show. Sometimes it's a joyous dog and pony show. Sometimes it's a tragic dog and pony show. It has all those qualities. It is a show! A *lila.*

A dance. The mystics have been saying this for thousands of years. This is a lila! It's a dance! It is the dance of Consciousness.

Does this fit with the ideas of the new physics?

The entire universe, everything in it, is notional, as opposed to material. Now this is what all the physicists are coming to, in the far fringes of theoretical physics and quantum mechanics. I don't understand it at all from the scientific perspective—but all matter is in fact notional. It exists only upon being perceived. Perception is what gives it definition, what gives it shape and form. Without being perceived, it doesn't exist as any *thing*. And thus the universe is revealed to be what the mystics have been saying all along—pure Consciousness. So this agency of measurement, the mind, this thought process, this perception is what gives this Wholeness qualities. The Wholeness is unbroken. The Wholeness itself is undifferentiated until there is some differentiation made. And that differentiation has to be made through a sentient organism of some kind. An *organism* with senses. So once there is an organism with senses that perceives something, that perception creates the universe. Or to say it more precisely, the object of perception and the object perceived arise simultaneously as phenomenality.

I would think that the universe creates that perception. That it happens at the same time.

Well they arise simultaneously. The perceiver and the perceived, subject and object, arise simultaneously.

That makes sense, yes. 'The Ten Thousand Things' arise together.

Exactly.

But it's a real paradox.

It is precisely that. It is a paradox. And the understanding of the sages is the resolution of that paradox. Or more precisely it is the dissolution of the paradox. Paradoxes can not be solved. You can not solve a koan. You can not solve a paradox. They can only be dissolved. And this dissolution comes by encompassing the paradox. The Understanding encompasses the paradox. And thus that which seemed to have two unresolvable aspects, irreconcilable aspects, is revealed to be two ends of the same stick. So what the Chinese call the 'Ten Thousand Things' are seen as an expression of the one indivisible Consciousness. The 'Ten Thousand Things' are seen not as divisions of Consciousness, but rather as eruptions of Consciousness. They're aspects of Consciousness. They're aspects of the One that cannot be broken. And thus it is seen that they are appearances, they are apparent separations. But the appearance of the separations is dependent upon something to make a distinction, without it there is Nothing.

♋   ♋   ♋

PREDESTINATION

Are you saying that everything is already written, like a script, predestined? Can we see the script?

The image that I prefer, is one Ramesh uses of a painting that is fifty miles long, upon which is inscribed everything that ever was and ever will be. All the events, all the reactions, all the nuances, everything is portrayed on this painting. In order for you as a perceiver—as a perceiving mechanism—to see this, because you're right next to it, time and space are required. You walk along it, and events are revealed, and are experienced as you proceed along, and you say, "This is happening." Now, if you were able to back up far enough to see the whole painting at once, you would see *it is all there!*

Now, the question of destiny, of predestination—is always from the standpoint or perspective of the perceiver that is right next to, and involved in a portion of What Is. As soon as the perception expands to embrace the Total; as soon as there is this perspective in which it is all seen as *being there* in the eternal present moment, then the question of predestination evaporates. The question of a script evaporates. IT ALL *IS!*

Then the only question that remains is, why is the painting as such? Can the mind comprehend that?

Why is the painting the way it is, and not some other way?

Right.

When you're asking, "Why?" about the characteristics or quality of What Is, there are infinite answers. If you want to take What Is and split it up into cause and effect relationship, which is to say, "Why? What caused this?"...pick an answer. Pick an answer that satisfies you. There are *hundreds* of them. Every religion, every cult, every sect has its answer. And they're easy to find. In fact there are information booths all over. They are well marked. The Christian Information booth has a cross on top. The Jewish booth has a six-pointed star on it. The Moslem one has a crescent moon and a little star. Stop in at any of them and you will find all the answers to, "Why?" you could ever want. Go any time. Many are manned twenty-four hours a day.

This teaching *points* to What Is in the eternal present moment. There is no dogma. There is no explanation.

There are no *reasons* given for anything. What Is, simply Is.

I'd like to understand the pointers more clearly. Like pointers to the Truth. You said that the mind could not possibly know its Source, because it's a character in the painting, and in order to know the painting it has to separate itself from the painting but it cannot. So it could not possibly know the Totality or the Source. On the other hand you talk about the Source; that all there is, is Consciousness. But your body-mind mechanism could not know that, so what's the pointer that allows you to talk about that? Is it an intuitive understanding?

In the most profound sense, it is not an understanding at all but rather it is that I *am* That. You *are* That. There's no question of separation from it to know it. In the separation is the *mis*-understanding, if you will. And thus when the separation ends, we call that Understanding. We say that the Understanding is intuitive, and therefore slightly more accurate than the intellectual understanding. The intellectual understanding is *clearly* in subject-object relationship. Intuitive Understanding is mushier. It's not as clearly defined. Therefore it more closely aligns with That which by its nature cannot be defined.

In this Advaita teaching, there seem to be two concepts which I find slightly paradoxical.

Only two? *(Loud laughter)*

One is: Everything is God's will, everything happening that's in this manifestation is the will of God and IS God. And there's also the concept that this is all an illusion, and—the illusion is not God. There is God, the fulcrum, if you like, and then there is the illusion, the pendulum. Does the fulcrum create the pendulum?

Yes. But the second concept you mention is not Advaita. The illusion, the manifestation is *not* independent of God. Do you remember the Kleenex trick? Well, the fulcrum is that from which all of the manifestation is extruded. If you unfold the Kleenex, the pendulum comes out, is fully extended, and that is the entire manifestation which is nothing but God. This is *all God*. This is *all Consciousness*. This is not *your* screw-up! This isn't some fake thing that exists outside of Reality. This illusion is Consciousness's illusion, not your illusion...except to the extent that you are Consciousness.

Excuse me if I stumble with this. This body-mind is God's, and the appearance of this body-mind which would like to think that it had created itself—in fact probably all its life has subtly been insisting that: 'I did it, I am the doer'—this person was created and is divine, because it is God.

Yes.

And yet God seeks to experience via limitation, as this manifestation, and may, if this destiny applies to 'this one,' then entertain itself by waking up and saying, "I'm not just this body, I am Everything, and Everything is me."My excuse for speaking is that there is the mysterious fact that 'this one' could actually know a Truth, beyond words, and wake to the fact of it. But for now I am still in the words of it. The words carry a potency that could awaken this being. Am I making myself clear?

You're making yourself clear, but what 'this one' would awaken to is the absence of anyone to Awaken. The Awakening is pure Isness. The notion that this manifestation is produced by Consciousness as an entertainment through which it can know the absence of itself and then seek knowledge of itself is certainly a very poetic and very beautiful way of putting things. And it is attractive to the human adult mind, to create a rationale which it can understand! But it is a story.

Ramesh uses this example all the time: he says, you take kids to the beach, drop them by the shore, and what do they do? They build a sandcastle. They take hours to build a sandcastle with turrets and moats and all kinds of things, and at the end of a couple of hours you say "OK kids, it's time to go." What do they do? They jump on it. Moosh it into *nothing*! And you say "Why did you *do that?* You spent all of that time creating this beautiful thing, and then in a few seconds you've destroyed all of your labors!"

And they'll look at you like you're nuts. Because what you're attempting to do, is put an adult human overlay, a rationale that makes sense to you, on this behavior. If you press them real hard, they'll say, "It's fun. We're doing it because it's fun." But they really don't think in those terms. They were simply doing.

Your question is an attempt to know and to order this little corner of reality that is your perception, into something that's comprehensible. And so when you're dealing with the Infinite, and Its manifestation, you say "OK, what the Infinite must be doing is what any rational adult human would do, who is writing a play or creating something. It's accomplishing something." And thus you ascribe those characteristics to Totality and say, "OK, that makes sense. I get it." And for a while anyway you sleep well at night, knowing you have it all figured out.

Just one little sort of niggling doubt...

Yes, that is what disturbs your sleep again! *(laughter)*

You talk about a 'me' identifying with the Totality and with Consciousness. Now where is this 'me' which can identify with Consciousness? There isn't a 'me' prior to Consciousness, is there? The 'me' that I might think I am, might think it's going to identify with Consciousness, but actually it's Consciousness identifying with this imaginary 'me.'

Correct, and when that identification as a separate doer evaporates, what is left is the default state. Yes. So linguistically I may have talked about the 'me' as if it exists...but that is the limitation of language.

But it's something that recently struck me: I was trying to identify with Consciousness, as if there was an 'I' prior to Consciousness, and there isn't.

No! And that's why *you* will never wake up; why *you* will never join with Consciousness; because you were never separate from *Consciousness* to be able to join with it.

But in a sense, I was trying to deify this I-amness separate from Consciousness, which is nonsense.

Yes, it is nonsense, but it is built into the structure of the perceptive mechanism, the subject-object relationship. You can't *think* outside of subject-object relationship. You can't *perceive* outside of subject-object relationship.

♋   ♋   ♋

SUBJECT AND OBJECT

It's amazing how this whole subject-object thing is going around for me; that what I think is a subject is actually an object if I can perceive it. Anything representing the sense of 'me' that I have is actually an object of perception, something that's being observed. Yet I can never quite get a hold of the thing that's observing it, somehow.

Right—because then it too would be an object. As soon as you 'get a hold of it,' it's objectified; and the only thing you can know is an object. The subject cannot know itself except as an object and then it is no longer the subject!

And this whole 'doing' thing—how can something that is merely a dream actually think that it's doing something?

You're kind of mixing metaphors there, because the dreamed object doesn't think it's a dream; it thinks it's something substantial. Even if it's an *object*, at least as an object it's substantial.

Yeah. But as a 'subjective object,' it's a doer. The sense that I have that I'm the doer is actually an object in Consciousness. So, there's no way that I can comprehend this thing, there's no way that I can see It, there's no way that I can find It...It is all of this?

You can't *find* It because you *are* It. The only way you could find *It* is by *not* being It and observing It...but there is nothing that is not It.

So then there's no solution or is it that this phenomenal being finally just realizes the fact that it doesn't really exist, but somehow the existence in phenomenality continues?

The realization is not by the phenomenal object. You're again thinking of the realization of the sage being the realization of the body-mind mechanism that is associated with the Knowing.

But it is truly not the Knowingness of that body-mind mechanism that we're referring to. The body-mind mechanism of the sage is just like any other body-mind mechanism, it is a conditioned object. The Knowing is pure Subjectivity.

But in that case there would be no phenomenality at all.

Well, that's where it gets real paradoxical.

So how does one become pure Subjectivity?

You've got to try *really* really hard. *(laughter)* And if you've not realized this lofty state of pure Subjectivity, it is simply because you have not tried hard enough.

Back to the drawing board.

And if you buy *that*, I've got a bridge I'd like to sell you as well!

♋   ♋   ♋

CAUSE AND EFFECT

Can I ask you about the understanding? You speak about the understanding being 'here.' Everybody sitting here has a certain level of understanding. I have this image of a pot of understanding being filled until the water flows over. But what was it for you? What actually happened at that moment to change the understanding that you had?

That which would understand, disappeared.

The seeker?

That which would understand. That which *would* *understand*. That which *had* the varying levels of understanding. That which went up the pendulum into a sense of impersonal doership, and then down the pendulum into a sense of greater personal doership; that was gone! And what was revealed was Understanding with a capital 'U.' (It's just a word!) It was in no way relative, it was in no way conditional, and it did not have any connection to subject-object relationship, a subject-object kind of understanding.

And this is brought about not as a result of any activity? Nothing can bring that about?

Well, now we're getting into the realm of cause and effect. Basically, you're asking, "Is that caused? Did something cause that understanding to happen, cause that event—albeit an impersonal one—to happen?" And from the point of view of a mega-understanding, the Universe is *uncaused*. It is *all here*. Everything IS. The script is written. The entire film is in the can. It is being *experienced* in time and space, through the senses, through the instruments of duality, which are the mind and its attendant senses. But the Understanding with a capital 'U,' *underlies* that; is both the source and the substance of that. And thus, it is not caused, because it is not within the realm of subject-object relationship. It is not in the realm of causality. Causality is a notion, is a way of ordering What Is. And it is very arbitrary. Ramesh uses this example—A man goes to the horse races in Bombay and puts a bet down on a horse, the horse wins, he wins money. And you say that that money came into his hands because the horse won the race. The horse winning the race caused the money to come into his hands. Now, an equally reasonable way to look at this is that in order for this money to be in his hands, so that some other event could happen—that his child would get the medical attention he needed so that he could go on to become the prime minister of India—in order for that event to happen, this fellow had to have that money. Therefore, the need for these subsequent events to happen *caused* the horse to win! That's not the way we normally view these events. But taking the events as a whole, that is another way of ordering, of *perceiving*, of making sense of these events.

Making sense of...?

Yes! The mind orders *What-Is* by taking a very few of the available events and creating a reality with them. If it were to attempt to absorb *all* of the events at once it would overload, it would fry! It is too huge an amount of data to absorb and process into order.

The occurrence of enlightenment appears to be something like the lottery in that it seems from this level to be random, or somewhat random.

From the personal standpoint, it is random. I can assure you it isn't a merit system. *(laughter)* That is most obvious in my case.

I guess I'm saying it, because it looks so random.

Sure, just so long as you understand that randomness is a notion that comes about from the standpoint of an individual. From the standpoint of the Understanding, where's randomness? There is no randomness. Everything Is. It's only 'random' from the standpoint of an individual.

♋   ♋   ♋

DEATH

When the 'body' part of the body-mind mechanism dies, can you tell us about the experience of the mind part? Does the mind necessarily die too, and if not what kinds of experiences does it have?

The body-mind organism is a single unit; they are not two separate components. The whole thing dissolves upon the dissolution or the death of either aspect. The ultimate effect can be likened to a toaster through which electricity flows. When it is unplugged, electricity remains, unchanged by the disappearance of the toaster.

Sometimes you hear people talk about other planes of existence; different places where, I guess, different conscious beings exist. Are these planes real?

They are as real as this plane is.

So in effect, we might have different kinds of body-mind complexes on different planes?

Sure. Why not?

Is death enlightenment?

No, death is the dissolution of the body-mind mechanism.

When there is nothing there, is that enlightenment?

No, enlightenment is the falling away of the sense of personal doership.

Can an animal be enlightened?

For an animal or baby there is no need for enlightenment because there is no sense of personal doership there, there is no sense of personal doership to fall away which is what enlightenment is. It can only happen once there is a sense of personal doership there. Now, at death you can say the sense of personal doership dissolves along with the body-mind mechanism.

Is death nothingness?

Nothingness for whom? Who are we talking about?

Is death like a deep sleep state where there are no thoughts?

Yes, in death as in deep sleep there is no 'one' there to experience the phenomenal manifestation. But the main point in all this is that what is experiencing through all of these body-mind mechanisms is Consciousness. So when one body-mind dies, the experiencer remains which is Consciousness. That is the only experiencer.

♋   ♋   ♋

REINCARNATION

Can we talk a bit about reincarnation?

Okay. It's fine with me.

I keep hearing different comments on that subject, and somebody said that you said there is no such thing as reincarnation.

I've been misquoted AGAIN! *(Laughter)* No, what I said is, that there is no *one* to reincarnate. There is no separate individual that reincarnates; because there is no separate individual incarnated in the first place. So, if you're not incarnated in the first place, it is very difficult for you to RE-incarnate. All there is is Consciousness, which expresses through these myriad forms. These myriad forms are created and destroyed in incredibly rapid succession, and in amazing diversity. So you can say that this Consciousness incarnates, and reincarnates, and reincarnates, and reincarnates and reincarnates and reincarnates. Every instant it is doing that, a thousand fold, a million fold; not only in human form, but in the forms of all kinds of objects, both sentient and not.

What about this concept of Samsara and, you know, getting off the wheel? Is that just a concept?

Yes. And if it appeals to you, fine, because what *I* just said to you was also just a concept. That description is conceptual, a pointer toward that Which Is. Now the pointer that I like the most, personally is Ramesh's description of the Universe. He wrote: "The Universe is uncaused, like a net of jewels in which each is *only* the reflection of all the others, in a fantastic interrelated harmony without end."

I'll repeat that, because I like it so much. *(laughter)*

> The Universe is uncaused,
> Like a net of jewels
> In which *each*—each jewel—
> Is *only* the reflection
> Of all the others.

Nothing has any independent existence. Each is only the reflection of everything else...

> In a fantastic interrelated harmony
> Without end.

Which is a very poetic and wonderful and beautiful way of saying: "It IS."

So you also could say that everything exists only as relationship?

Yes. You could certainly say that.

Accepting that all phenomenality is merely like a dream, does reincarnation exist within the context of that dream?

The question again, is, "What reincarnates? Is there something separate that you are other than the Consciousness of which 'you' are made?"

No.

Then what reincarnates is Consciousness. It continuously reincarnates. It reincarnates as you, It reincarnates as him, It reincarnates as her, and there's a constant rising and falling of this energy of Consciousness as It expresses within phenomenality in all manner of things.

So then, what is past-life regression or memories of past lives?

Within each body-mind mechanism there are memories. They exist within the brain, and when a body-mind mechanism dissolves, those memories, you could say, go back into the pool of Consciousness. There's nowhere else that they can go, because all there is is Consciousness. Out of this Consciousness, new mechanisms are formed, and within the new mechanisms those memories may arise. If the new mechanism has a sense of personal doership, it will believe, "I am this thing. I am this body, I am this mind, and these are my thoughts. Therefore, if I have these thoughts of a previous life it must be that *I* have lived in a previous life."

This past weekend in Atlanta I told the sandcastle story, and one gentleman said, "So...what you're telling me is that we're God's *sandcastles?* " I replied, "Yes, that is *exactly* the case. We *are* God's sandcastles! And He's invested enormous time and attention and gone to great pains to create each of these separate mechanisms, each of which have different fingertips, different retinal patterns—each one absolutely unique. Each organism is made up of the same materials—all of them made of the exact same basic nucleic acids, all the same genetic material, yet each and every one of them is unique. Each one of them is created, exists for a little while, and is then 'mooshed' like the sandcastle. And that's just how it is." So of course the adult intellect asks, "Why? Why am I here? Why am I going to be mooshed? Couldn't I be one of the *non*-mooshed ones? *(laughter)* If I become enlightened, will I then be *unmooshable?*" *(laughter)* What a seductive premise! "Wow, I can get free from this body that's going to get mooshed and still maintain my individuality!" But if you know that you're sand rather than a sandcastle, then it doesn't matter what form that sand takes. The fact that it builds up into a human shape or is mooshed back down into the beach doesn't matter.

In holding the view of oneself as the basic irreducible substance rather than as its manifestation, it would seem to follow that you could always become something else.

Exactly...and you *will*. So the *sand* can be said to reincarnate, but the sand*castle* does *not* reincarnate.

It's my understanding from Ramesh that even though, let's say, the sand would reincarnate from one particular castle, Consciousness can also bring sand from another sandcastle and mix it in with that, so then the 'reincarnated' sandcastle would think that it was part of both previous castles. So maybe that's why people recounting past lives sometimes feel that they've previously been more than just one person, or part of several persons, within the same lifetime.

Yes of course they would be 'mixed.' The thing about past lives is that they have to do with memories. Memories exist as part of the Whole. When an organism dies, its memories or contents of mind are no longer differentiated from the Whole. So out of that, memories may show up in some other body-mind mechanism. If that mechanism considers himself to be the doer and he has a memory of some past action, then he'll say, "That was *my* action! *I* did that back then!"

♋   ♋   ♋

MEMORY, TIME AND THE ETERNAL NOW

When we speak of memory, it seems that the memory of our entire life dictates our reactions to things at the very moment at which they take place. The thing I struggle with is that I have been given memories of past lives, and yet a part of me is much more comfortable with: "What was, Is; what is, Is; and what will be, Is." How do memories of past lives fit into that equation if everything is a spontaneous happening in the Eternal Now?

Well, we need to back up one level of magnification to understand the answer to that, which is to say that all is here Now, including the memories and the reactions to the memories. It's all here in the Eternal Present Moment. But in order for memories to be experienced, they have to be experienced in space and time. Anything experienced in space and time within a linear context necessarily registers a cause-and-effect relationship between those two factors. But there is nothing inconsistent about a particular memory being in itself an appearance of cause and effect while simultaneously being a part of everything which is there in the spontaneity of the Eternal Present Moment. There is no conflict from the point of view of Totality; there is, however, tremendous conflict in trying to resolve those two things—memory and spontaneity—from the point of view of the identified individual. They are irreconcilable, in fact. Another paradox.

So when the 'me' drops, then there is no more question regarding how to reconcile them?

That is precisely the case. When the 'me' drops, there is no longer a thinking process to extend What Is into space and time. There is pure Isness as a reality rather than as a speculative concept or a belief held by a separate being. They are two very different things.

So then we have no purpose, per se, other than to live and coexist, and that's very freeing! (laughter)

It certainly is!

♋   ♋   ♋

WHAT USE IS THIS TEACHING?

If there is nothing we can do to get enlightened, what is the value of hearing this teaching?

For me, the value—and value is measured in very personal terms—for me the value of hearing this teaching was that my life became easier. This teaching became part of me, intellectually, and phenomenally. The response—the effect upon this body-mind mechanism—was that my life, my reactions to things, became easier. Acceptance of *what is, in the moment,* became more frequent. The thought would arise as I reacted to something, that this reaction is part of the functioning of Totality. This reaction could not be otherwise. This reaction is simply *happening*. And that recognition cut off the horizontal involvement of the mind, of the thinking process, which analyzes, speculates, considers and judges every thought and action. The cutting off of that process brings one right back to the moment—brings one right back to *here*—brings one right back to the present; and the present is where life is.

This is the contact point for experiencing one's connection with Totality, for seeing the Divine in the ordinary. This connection is always there. There is no disconnection. There has never been any disconnection. All is One. All is God. The experience of disconnection, the experience of separateness, is removed *here* in the Eternal Present Moment.

The value of this teaching is in *that,* not in getting you enlightened. This teaching has no effectiveness in terms of getting you enlightenment because *you* are *never* going to get enlightened! And this is not because of some limitation on your part, or on the part of the teaching, but rather because NO ONE IN THE ENTIRE HISTORY OF THE UNIVERSE has ever been enlightened. There are no enlightened people.

Enlightenment is an *impersonal event* in phenomenality. The effect of that impersonal event in phenomenality upon a particular body-mind mechanism is quite variable. However, it does not produce a superman.

Ramesh was the only person that I ever heard talk about that. I'm sure there are plenty of others who have, and do, and will, but in my limited experience he was the only one I ever encountered to get to *that crux* of this question of enlightenment, and 'who' is enlightened, and what does one 'get' out of this enlightenment deal. He continues to talk about this at ten o'clock every morning at his place in Bombay. He talks about just this: that there *is* no personal enlightenment, that *you're* not going to get enlightened, that when enlightenment happens through the body-mind mechanism, that the net effect of this event is that the body-mind mechanism through which it happens knows that there is no such thing as personal enlightenment!

Now, this helps to explain why right now (April of 1999) there are only about thirty people at Ramesh's daily talks. He's been talking regularly about this for twelve years, and for several years before that to the occasional person who came by. He's got ten books in print in a dozen languages and there are just thirty people there! There will be a few more when the weather's better and it's more pleasant to be in Bombay! Then the numbers will skyrocket to fifty or sixty! Obviously, this is not a message that is very attractive to many seekers. The notion that you are NOT going to get what you want, doesn't sell. What sells is, that if you just *do it right*, if you just perfect it, if you work hard at it, if you're diligent enough, YOU WILL GET IT!

And I'll help you! *(laughter)*.

But it wasn't only the intellectual teaching that Ramesh put forth, that was of benefit to me personally—and after all, who do I really care about? *(laughter)*—but in Ramesh's presence, because there was Resonance, because there was this connection, *in the Resonance, in the connection,* something very profound happened. And it is really very difficult to talk about, because the words are so limiting, they are so inadequate to the task of describing what happens in that connection between the Guru and disciple. It was a consummate blessing for me, as a body-mind mechanism who considered himself separate and a doer, one who was caught up in this web of desires and disappointments, and all of that. For me, that relationship, that connection, was the most profound experience of my life. And you never know where it's going to happen, or with whom. But when it does, it is absolute magic.

♋   ♋   ♋

A rock
Allowed to remain on the ground
Weighs nothing.
Ram Tzu

♋   ♋   ♋

Each Individual Human
Is a mask God wears
To express himself.
Masks are crucial.
Without them there could
Be no play.
As there would be no way
To differentiate the characters.

But occasionally
God wears a mask
That is nearly transparent
And the observant theatre-goer
Catches a glimpse of the Infinite.
Wayne

♋   ♋   ♋

Just because the spiritual master lets you call him
by his first name doesn't mean he isn't dangerous.

♋   ♋   ♋

Whither shall I go from thy spirit? or whither shall I flee
from thy presence?
If I ascend up into heaven, thou art there: if I make my bed
in hell, behold, thou art there.
If I take the wings of the morning, and dwell in the utter-
most parts of the sea;
Even there shall thy hand lead me, and thy right hand shall
hold me.

Psalms 139:9

♋   ♋   ♋

The first step. . . shall be to lose the way.
Galway Kinnell

THREE

THE BEGINNING OF SEEKING

SEEKERS ARE A RARE BREED

What brings you here today?

You were highly recommended.

Really? What did they tell you? It just interests me sometimes how people are attracted to come here. I mean, it interests me how *I* got here! It seems absolutely ludicrous to me that I should be here doing this, so I'm often curious as to whether anybody else shares my bewilderment and delight that this is even *happening! (laughter)*

It just seems to me the perfect place to be. If I had to choose between this and whatever else I might be doing, like working or watching television...this is perfect.

Now isn't it interesting that you would consider this to be perfect? I would dare say that there are other people walking by on the street who, if you were to stop them and say, "There is a perfect moment happening in there," would respond with, "Oh? Are you having sex in there? Or are you finding some way to make money or watching a cool TV program in there?" You would then say, "No, we're talking about Consciousness. We're talking about our True Nature. We're discussing our Oneness with God," and they would think: "What is *she* on? *(laughter)* That doesn't sound like a 'perfect' afternoon to *me!* "

We should try taking that line about 'the perfect moment' out on Sunset Boulevard in Hollywood.

Right. "Hey, Sailor, you want a hot concept?" *(laughter)* But do you see what I mean? Isn't it unusual that you should consider this to be the most perfect place that you could possibly be, yet someone else wouldn't set foot in here if you *paid* them? How did this happen to you? I mean, presumably you weren't born with an interest in Advaita philosophy, this *has* been a process for you.

It's still a process, but it's kind of like arriving at a place that I always knew existed. And then when I came upon it, I felt, "Oh, this is comfortable." So although I still 'move along,' whenever I recognize an opportunity to come back to that place, I take it.

Now this quality of suspecting that there is some 'place' out there—even though you might not know what 'It' is, but just feeling a desire for It, knowing that It exists—is not something that happens to most people. It only happens to people whom we call 'seekers.' And my presumption in regard to the specific point at which the thought or feeling arose that there *is* something out there and It's *not* material, is that *you* didn't *cause* that arising to happen. You were simply going along your natural course in life, and suddenly the feeling *arose*—whether at the age of two years old, or fourteen, or thirty—that there's something more, that something we'll call 'spiritual' exists. Now this is what the sage Ramana Maharshi calls the point at which your 'head goes into the tiger's mouth,' the jaws close, and there is no escape. You're now a seeker, and this seeking carries you forward. It makes you decide to drive across town to hear someone talk about Consciousness rather than to a fashion show, or to a seminar on multilevel marketing, or to a health spa, or to any one of the thousand other places that you could potentially be this afternoon. Being a seeker means that when somebody tells you that there's a guy in Hermosa Beach talking spirituality and there may be some 'juice' there, you say, "Let's *go!* "

I'm sure by now you've experienced going someplace and meeting somebody who gives a talk and having a very positive reaction to that, and then going to a friend and saying, "That teacher I heard is just *amazing!* You've got to come and hear this guy. He's extraordinary. You sit there and you become utterly transformed! It's the most unbelievable experience you can possibly have." And your friend says, "Oh yeah? Well count me *in*— let's go!" And he goes with you, sits down and listens for a while, and says, "What the hell is *this?* "

That quality which I call 'Resonance' either occurs between two body-mind mechanisms, or it doesn't. And when there is Understanding happening through one of those mechanisms, and there is Resonance between them, there is what is called a Guru-Disciple relationship. That occurs *only* in the presence of this Resonance;

without it, the room can be filled to the walls with so-called enlightened people, and you'll walk right by. There has to be that Resonance.

It used to drive me nuts! The second time I met my Guru, Ramesh at a talk he gave up in the Hollywood Hills, he came in and sat down with the four or five of us there, and I had the most incredible experience with him, one that was totally unexpected. It was so profound, and so revelatory, that I assumed it would be accessible to anybody who was there. So, I brought my friends to hear him, and they said, "Oh, nice little Indian guy. He's cute. Very pleasant." But *nothing*! Ramesh was up there in the Hollywood Hills for two-and-a-half months, talking every day, twice a day, and hundreds of people came to hear him. Yet, most of them—the overwhelming majority—never came back.

It is like this: You go to a well, you've got a bucket with a rope attached to it, and the rope is ten feet long. You throw the bucket into the well and you haul it back up, and you get a beautiful bucket of cool, clear water. You call your friends, tell them all about it and they come. They've got buckets with ropes that are eight feet long, and they throw in their buckets and say, "What are you talking about? This well is *dry*! There's nothing here, man."

♋   ♋   ♋

LOOKING FOR FREEDOM

So, how do you find yourself here today?

Well, I'm from Fairfield, Iowa. That might tell you something. I heard about you from a friend there.

So presumably, you've had plenty of experience and background in Transcendental Meditation. How has the interest in Advaita developed?

Through Gangaji. I really don't know much, though.

But you're interested. Do you know what it is you're interested in?

Freedom.

Mm-hmm. What does 'freedom' mean to you?

Not being caught up in the world-dream.

Then presumably you know the by-product of being 'caught up.'

Suffering.

Well, I certainly couldn't blame you for not wanting to suffer. I assume you've tasted this freedom.

I've had a glimpse.

The good news and the bad news about the glimpses is that they keep you going. Depending on the day, that's either good news or bad news. And there are some very good days along the path—very 'high times.' But as with everything that operates within phenomenality, it's dualistic in nature. So for every high, there is a corresponding low. Of course, the seductive promise in the idea of 'personal enlightenment' is that you can have the 'highs' all the time. That's the way I imagined it. *(laughter)* I had tasted 'Oneness,' and I wanted more. I wanted that experience all the time. I didn't want to be hanging around flip-flopping like a fish out of water. I wanted to be 'awake' all the time. The notion and expectation that I could be 'there' all the time, without having the corresponding feeling of being 'not there,' was very seductive to me.

Fortunately, I met Ramesh reasonably early on in my search (at least in my conscious search) and he disabused me of the notion that 'I' was going to get enlightenment. He informed me that the experience I had, which was impersonal in nature but was claimed by me as a personal experience, was not enlightenment. And that was kind of a shocker, because that experience of Oneness was probably the most profound experience that I'd ever had. There was something deeply true about it, and deeply meaningful, because this feeling of unity is the most fulfilling, the deepest, the most completing experience that the body-mind mechanism can have. And what Ramesh finally got through to me was that that experience could be considered to be a taste, a look over the fence, or one of a number of things, but that it wasn't *It*. He said that the awakening that the sages were talking about was of an entirely different dimension. The Ultimate Awakening was one in which the one who was going to enjoy an experience of awakening was in fact not there, and thus the bliss that was talked about was not a personal bliss. It was the absence—the utter and complete absence—of anyone to be blissful.

Now I can't say I bought this entirely at first. Because even though I paid intellectual lip-service to that being the truth, and I trusted Ramesh to be pointing me in the right direction, there was still present here a sense of personal doership—someone who felt that he was the doer. And as long as the 'Divine Hypnosis' is there in which I consider myself to be a separate individual acting, it is incomprehensible, it is impossible, for this Impersonality (which is What Is, which is the underlying Totality of Being) to be experienced. But the nice thing about that whole teaching, that whole process, was that through it, the seeking started to slip away. The wanting enlightenment, wanting freedom, wanting the bliss, just started to fade. And it started to fade with the understanding that everything was happening in accordance with the will of God, or the play of Consciousness, or the dance of Shiva, or whatever you want to call it. The understanding deepened that everything in the manifestation was being carried out on its own—including all the thoughts, all the actions, everything that was happening through this particular body-mind.

Just hearing that was enough?

Oh, I had to hear that for a while. *(laughter)* Over, and over, and over, and over again.

Still, there was no conscious trying to let go of the desire for seeking the truth.

Oh, there was some of that for awhile, and then even that got kind of boring. Even that was revealed as being just another slightly more sophisticated type of doership. And then you can couch it in really sophisticated terms and say: "I'm not doing; I'm letting"—as if a 'letting' isn't a 'doing'! It can get very sophisticated. *(laughter)*

♋   ♋   ♋

WORTH A SIXTY MILE DRIVE

So, what were you told that would induce you to get into your car and drive sixty miles to come here?

That you are enlightened...

Yes. So? Even assuming for a moment that this were true, you could tell lots of people in Laguna Hills that little piece of information, yet they would not get in their car!

I'm one of those fools who, if I hear, or think, or suspect that there is anybody who has enlightenment, I'll go there and see them. Plus, I'm curious. I have to see if what I was told is true! (laughter)

How would you know?

That's hard to answer in words. You can kind of point to it or allude to it, but it's really a feeling.

Lots of people come here, and if what I say agrees with what they already know and believe is true, then they say, "This guy really knows what he's talking about. He is okay!" *(laughter)* And if what I'm saying does not agree with what they already know or believe to be the truth, they say, "He's full of shit," and they go on down the road.

I could probably do either one, but there's stuff in between the lines too. I'm looking for that.

Yes, there is, and that is what I call 'Resonance.' And if there is that Resonance, then it doesn't matter what's being said.

Right.

This whole concept of 'Enlightened Beings' gets real tricky, because there aren't any 'Enlightened Beings.' Enlightenment could be said to be a shift in identification from the body-mind mechanism to the Totality. But the body-mind mechanism continues, and it may very well continue to function as it always has. And the fact that this impersonal event of Understanding or Awakening has happened through a particular body-mind mechanism—not to it, but through it—is of no concern to that which Knows. Furthermore, That which would consider itself to be enlightened is gone. That which identifies with the body-mind mechanism as the doer, and as one who could become enlightened, is gone.

It's really kind of funny, and that's why my Guru, Ramesh, says, "If you have the choice between enlightenment and a million dollars, take the million dollars! Because if you get the million dollars, there will be somebody there to enjoy the million dollars; but if you get enlightenment, there's no one there to enjoy the enlightenment!" It's ironic because the seeking is done nominally by someone who considers himself to be a seeker. The seeking is done through a body-mind mechanism that considers itself to be a doer who is going to do something, and thus get something. And even when there is an intellectual comprehension and an intellectual understanding that this is not the case, there's still the sense of personal doership on the part of the seeker. Until it's removed, it's there.

What is there after it's removed? Is there still an awareness?

Of course there is! There is still a perfectly functioning mechanism with thoughts and reactions. And it eats, and it shits, and it makes love, and it does all the things that it did before. But there is no longer a sense of personal doership associated with the action.

Okay, now I get it.

Then the sixty-mile drive was worth it! *(laughter)*

So it comes in glimpses?

Glimpses happen, intellectual understandings happen, intuitive understandings by the individual happen—all as part of the functioning of Totality, all as part of this movement of seeking that happens through this body-mind mechanism. And seeking does not happen through most body-mind mechanisms. You've probably determined, when talking to your friends and family, that they're not interested in this. This is not a viable interest according to most people. What are the usual concerns? That you get a job, you get a mate, that you accumulate a certain amount of wealth, that you take care of your responsibilities, maybe travel a little bit, you recreate, you watch television and go to an occasional movie, watch a sporting event on television and maybe go to the ballpark every once in a while. "That's what you should do!" they say.

Why would we do that? (laughter)

Spoken like a true seeker.

♋   ♋   ♋

LOOKING FOR TRUTH

How do you find yourself here today?

Well, I am very interested in Truth. And my heart has been telling me to come to California for a time. So when I heard that there were going to be so many people from the Advaitic tradition here in L.A., I decided to come.

I see.

So that's why I'm here.

So, when you say you're interested in Truth, what exactly do you mean by that?

Well I feel that the only purpose in my life is to know the Truth, and to be used by Truth. In a way, coming to hear people speak Truth supports that. But it may also be an illusion. I still have a concept that the Truth of who I am is outside of me, or can somehow be found outside of me...

Or inside of you for that matter!

That's a good point. Yeah. So I came. I don't really know why I'm here, but I felt drawn to be here.

Ah-ha. It's interesting. That is exactly the plight, if you will, of the seeker: that there is an arising of this desire, this sense of wanting to know your true nature...the Truth. How long have you been interested in this subject?

A long time. Fifteen years I'd say, but really giving my life to it...maybe two years .

So do you remember what happened fifteen years ago, to change you from a presumably fairly normal, average, everyday kind of person into a seeker?

Well, I had this belief that money was who I was and if I had that I'd be complete. So I pursued that, and when I achieved that, I realized, "No, that's not it."

Damn!

Yeah.

It had such promise. *(laughs)*

It was so controllable, or so it seemed.

Yeah.

So then I thought, well the Truth must exist somewhere in my heart. I began a spiritual search then, and I moved into a meditation community in Iowa, and began this study of Truth. Do you want to hear the rest of this story?

Sure!

Okay. So after a time in the meditation community, I was sitting in meditation and got a real clear calling, which was shocking to me because nothing had happened like that before, to start a business. So I thought, "Oh! Okay. I'm supposed to integrate my business experience and my spiritual understanding." And so I started a business that I could never make succeed, which was such a great gift because my whole self-definition on the ego level was, "I am the successful doer."

Ah-ha.

I completed that business about two years ago, and I realized then that I had caught myself again in my ego definition, and decided I was going to just devote myself totally to Truth. So since then that's what I've been doing. Whatever that looks like.

I'm sure it changes faces.

Yes.

So what is it, do you think, that turned you from a successful businesswoman into a seeker? I mean there are lots of successful businesswomen around who reach that point where they achieve material success, have plenty of money, etc., etc., and they go on with the rest of their lives. Maybe they start doing some social work or join the country club, or make some more money or whatever. But they never make the transition into looking for something as bizarre as union with God.

Really?

Really. *(laughs)*

You know it seems to me and it is, of course, just a belief that everything we do is about seeking.

Well that is true. But it's not necessarily a spiritual seeking. Generally you reach a point of having achieved in one area, and if that leaves you still unfulfilled, you find a new area to provide you with the fulfillment that you think you will get.

Yes.

So most people, don't end up in places like this! Really! How do you think that that happened with you?

Well, I don't know. I could make up a story about it. In business I had some experiences where I recognized that there was such a deeper level of Truth operating in what I was doing that I didn't understand, but I knew was there. And so I wanted to explore that more. To get more, probably. Initially, it was certainly out of that motivation. I could say it was that. But I don't know, I think it's just that I knew there was a Truth to life that I wasn't fully connected with. I always knew that somehow. I think we all know that. That's my opinion. I knew it when I was a child, certainly. Very clearly.

Yes.

And I just assume everybody knows that...well children certainly know it.

♋   ♋   ♋

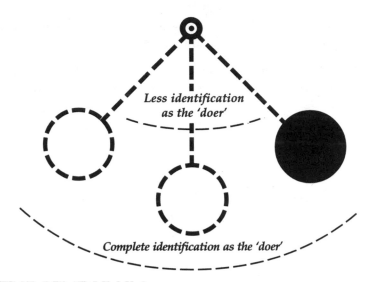

*Less identification
as the 'doer'*

Complete identification as the 'doer'

THE PENDULUM

Well, I have a model—a visual aid, as it were—
that speaks to precisely this process. Basically the model
is that this movement is like a pendulum movement, the
movement between polaric opposites, between happiness
and sadness, between satisfaction and dissatisfaction, between getting what you want and not getting what you
want, between health and sickness. Life is a movement
between these polaric opposites. And it's continual.

If you're identified completely as the doer of your
actions then you're riding at the very tip of this pendulum, such that when things are going well, you're
ecstatic, and when things are going poorly, you're miserable. When you're healthy, you're happy. When you're
sick, it's horrendous. When you're getting what you
want, you're delighted. And when you're not getting
what you want, you're absolutely miserable. This is the
state of most people. There's just this huge swinging back
and forth between the polaric opposites.

Now, with some individuals, at some point in this process, there comes a moment, and they may not even recognize it, but a moment comes when there is a sense that maybe, just perhaps, I am not the center of the universe. Perhaps I am not the end all and be all of everything. Maybe there's something more. Maybe there is something operative in the universe other than me. And that is the point at which there is a dislocation from this total sense of personal doership, from the sense that, "I'm the one who's doing this." That's the point that the sage, Ramana Maharshi, says, "Your head goes into the tiger's mouth, the jaws close, and there's no escape." You are now a seeker. So begins this process of seeking to know what is the functional element in the universe. "If I'm not it, if...maybe...just *(laughs)* assuming for a millisecond that maybe I'm not it, then what is?" And that begins this process of seeking, which is a process of disidentification as the doer.

The increased sense of disidentification as the doer is, figuratively speaking, a movement up the pendulum shaft. Now the same stuff happens in life. Good stuff happens, bad stuff happens. But notice, if you're identified up the shaft, your subjective movement in this swing—the way it seems—is much smaller. You are moved in a much smaller arc, because there isn't this sense that I am doing it. There is more of a sense that this is all happening, that I'm an instrument through which this is happening.

And occasionally, on your really good days, like the *really* good days, there's a movement to the very top of the pendulum shaft, and then life and living is going on, and you are totally unmoved by it all. There is pure witnessing of *all* that's happening. There is a sense (and I know that you've experienced it), a sense of impersonal connection with everything, and in it the Oneness is palpable. That all this life and living is just going on. It's going on perfectly. It's going on precisely the way it's supposed to be going on. There's utter and complete peace. And it doesn't get any better than that! That's as good as it gets, phenomenally speaking. You are *one* with the universe! What could be better than that?

This experience may last five minutes, or ten minutes, or a day, or a week. Maybe it'll last a month, or six months. If you're very, very lucky it could last quite a while. But what's crucial to understand is that this experience at the very top of the pendulum is an experience *in phenomenality*, even though it's impersonal. It is still an experience. It has substance. It has characteristics. You can say it's great. Therefore, there's something there. That means it exists in phenomenality. And anything that exists in phenomenality has one basic quality to it: it's subject to change, it *will* change. It carries within itself the very seed of its opposite.

And the change is tragic. The change is awful. What is revealed is that this is, in fact, a greased pendulum shaft. You find that you have slid back down into involvement. And now you're swinging again. Now you're suffering again. Now you have the conviction that you're the doer again, despite all the intellectual premises to the contrary. I mean, you've been to all the talks, you've read all the books, you know that you're not the doer, but the experience is of personal doership. The experience is *I'm doing it.*

Now that experience, having just come from a state of impersonal witnessing of All That Is, is *awful*. It is experienced as a fall from Grace. The great Christian mystic, St. John of The Cross, describes this as the long, dark night of the soul. He had the experience of being one with God, and he wrote about it very eloquently. He was connected. He was at one with all that was. And then he slid down the pendulum shaft. He didn't put it that way, *(laughter)* but that was his experience. What he actually said was that God had abandoned him. He felt as if he had been *abandoned* by God. And he went into a horrible depression. He was absolutely nonfunctional. Today they lock you up for a few days, give you some pills, and send you on your way. But then, they didn't have those luxuries.

The Impersonal Awakening is *not* this point at the top of the pendulum shaft. That is a point in phenomenality. That is a point that's subject to change. There will always be movement in and out of that state. It is a state in phenomenality. It is subject to change. What all the sages have been *pointing* towards is the quantum shift and it's a total paradigm shift, from identification *anywhere* on the pendulum shaft, to identification at the fulcrum.

Now the fulcrum is that upon which the pendulum *moves*. The fulcrum is *crucial* to all the movement. Without it there's no movement. But the thing about the fulcrum is that nothing *happens* there. There is no movement there. There is nothing *going on*. There is no subject-object relationship, which is what movement is. There is just the Oneness. In the Oneness there is no *feature*. If there is no feature, there's nothing to experience, and no one to experience it. And that can be said to be the state of the sage.

How we doing so far?

Beautifully.

Cool. (laughter)

Regarding your pendulum analogy—when that which brought you on the path decides to bring you up to the fulcrum, you could be really anywhere on the pendulum at that time, couldn't you? You wouldn't necessarily have to be near the top or whatever, because when that identification as a separate entity falls off, it just falls off, right?

That's correct.

If you merge totally with the Source, though, then supposedly you're free of coming back.

If only the one all-pervasive, undivided Source exists, who 'becomes free'? Who 'comes back'?

♋   ♋   ♋

LOOKING FOR
BETTER CONCEPTS

Are we meeting for the first time today?

Yes.

And how did you hear about this?

A friend.

And what did this friend tell you to induce you to come here?

He said, to come check it out.

Did he tell you there would be dancing girls?

No. (laughs) May have gotten here sooner! He said there was a gathering and described you briefly, very briefly, and said I needed to come down and see for myself.

Tall, good looking, full head of hair. *(laughs)*

I don't know about the full head of hair.

What do you do for a living?

I'm in marketing. I'm a partner in a computer marketing company.

Software? Hardware?

Hardware.

Do you often find yourself in gatherings such as this?

Well, not for a long time. I grew up in an environment where my mom took me to gatherings such as this quite often. But it has been many, many years.

Do you want to be enlightened?

I don't know, really, what that means, but I am interested in Truth, about myself and others, and overall existence. So if that's what enlightenment means, knowing more about that, and becoming more in touch with that, then yeah.

This Truth business is really an interesting one. Because, as Lao Tzu so succinctly pointed out in the first line of the Tao Te Ching: "The Tao that can be named is not the true Tao." I would translate that to mean that the truth that can be spoken about is not the Truth. Now, what we're doing here is we're trading concepts. Perhaps those concepts may point in the direction of the Truth, but the understanding is that the Truth is not intellectually accessible.

You can feel it though. I mean, one concept versus another feels right, and when you can be in touch with that, then you know that it's the right direction. And sometimes you have to come to gatherings like these to hear different concepts. Maybe a concept you're holding on to feels less right than one that's put forth here. Then you can let go of that and maybe start to embrace a better one, and hopefully that will lead to an even better one.

Ah-ha. Well that is certainly the process of seeking, where you go from one discipline to another, one set of concepts, notions, directions, pointers, to another. The result of that process, of course, is quite variable. We like to think in terms of it being a progression, and that we will advance from a minimal understanding to a little bit greater, to a little bit greater. And with a lot of effort and arduous concern, we're going to climb this mountain. And when we get to the pinnacle, there will be Peace, there will be Truth, revealed. And I prefer, really, the image of *(pause, searching for a reading)*...ah, here we are:

> You think of the Path
> As a long arduous climb
> Up the mountain.
>
> You concede there may be
> Many paths
> But you're sure
> All have the same
> Exalted goal.
>
> Ram Tzu knows this...
> There are many Paths.
> Like streams
> They flow effortlessly
> (though not necessarily painlessly)
> Down the mountain.
>
> All disappear
> Into the desert sands below

What do you mean by the disappearing into the desert sands part of that?

The seeking ends in the dissolution, not only of all of the concepts and the seeking, but with the dissolution of the seeker. And it is, you can say, a merging with the Oneness, a falling away of the sense of twoness. Now, having said all that, none of that is from a personal standpoint. You see, enlightenment is an impersonal event. It is an impersonal Understanding. It is an impersonal Awakening. There isn't anyone who has merged with the Oneness. There is only Oneness. What is absent is the sense, the identification as twoness. It is not the absence of twoness, because twoness is a concept that arises out of the Oneness. This whole manifestation is *notionally* twoness. It is an expression of Oneness into twoness. What the Chinese call, "The Ten Thousand Things," that arise out of the One. But they are never separate from the One. They are never anything but the One. They are merely an appearance of separation. They are *aspects* of the One.

And they forget.

Yes! The human ones. They believe themselves (some of them, the ones over the age of two and a half, or so) to be independent entities separate from Totality.

As soon as they believe that, they begin their striving towards, or yearning?

No, not necessarily. Many people go throughout their entire lives absolutely convinced that they're separate beings. There's no yearning that arises at all. There's no sense, "Oh, I have to find my True Nature." That happens only with seekers. Now, if you hang around with seekers all the time then everybody you know has that yearning. That's your culture. That's your environment. That seems like the way everybody is. But, I promise you *(laughs)* that is not the way everybody is. The seeking only happens through a relatively few body-mind mechanisms. And I use the term, 'body-mind mechanisms' to refer to all of these instruments of Totality which are a combination of body and mind. Infused in the human ones, at age approximately two and a half, was a sense of personal doership. This was not a life-style choice by the two and a half-year-old. This was something that arose! This was something that is part of this entire play. It's not a cosmic fuck-up. It's part of What Is. The fact that you have a sense of personal doership is neither God's screw up, nor yours. It's part of the functioning of Totality. And the fact that you are a seeker, that you're examining this, that you are looking at this, that you're beginning to question whether this is actually true, is also part of the functioning of Totality.

So why are we here doing all this?

I know why all of us are here today. None of us got a better offer. It's pretty sad, isn't it? This is the best we could do. *(laughter)*

But I am really glad I didn't get a better offer!

It's nice when you feel like you've landed in precisely the right place, rather than, "Oh I shouldn't be here. This isn't right. I want to be some place else." Because that's suffering. The sense that things should be other than they are, is suffering.

ඉ   ඉ   ඉ

WAYNE'S SEEKING

When you look at all the millions of searchers, and how few are self-realized...

Yes.

So how did you earn that?

Let's see...I was a very nice guy. *(laughs)* I worked very hard. I was very earnest. I was kind and loving to all. You're not buying this are you? *(laughter)* It's Grace!

It's Grace?

It's pure Grace. I was a pig for much of my life. *(laughs)* Give me more. Period. Give me more. I want more. More is not enough. There's not enough booze. There's not enough drugs. There's not enough sex. There's not enough money. There's not enough strokes of recognition. There's not enough! So, I will do whatever I need to do to get more. And so I was not a nice person. I was not helping others. I was not being generous. I was not being kind. I was not being loving. I was out there for me. And that's incredibly painful. That's a very horrible way to live. Not one that you would choose if you had a choice. And it's one that kills many people younger than me. But for me, for this body-mind mechanism, there was Grace. Go figure. So that's how I did it. So if you want to follow my 'path' you'd better start drinking. *(laughter)* You have a lot of catching up to do. You've got nineteen years of hard living still to go!

Well does it count that I lived with an alcoholic father?

No! I didn't live with an alcoholic father.

But you said that you were ready to go to any lengths. I think that maybe going to any lengths is what allowed the Grace to happen. That was it. Okay?

No. I had nothing to do with it.

No?

No. It just happened. It was another event in phenomenality. An impersonal one. I didn't do anything. This body-mind called Wayne is an instrument. This is flesh and bone, connected to a nervous system, associated with a brain. It's a body and a mind that has certain genetic characteristics, combined with subsequent conditioning. And that's what responds. That is how actions happen through this body-mind mechanism, you see. And so all of the actions, all of the years of alcoholism and drug addiction, the years of being not nice, if you will, were a condition of this body-mind mechanism at that time. Then there was a change. That change was not caused by this body-mind mechanism.

And what was extraordinary, you see, is I had been addicted for nineteen years. Well I'd only probably been addicted for seventeen, but I'd been at it for nineteen years. One night, at the end of a four day run, a binge, I'm lying in bed, and the clear recognition and acknowledgment comes with absolute certainty, that I can't do this any more. That it's over! I felt it go. I physically felt that obsession which was integral to my whole being, go. It just left. It was gone. I mean, I was someone who woke up in the morning, poured rum in my coffee, drank through the entire day, had to score a couple of grams of cocaine every couple of days, just to make it through the week, and that had gone! And I didn't want it to go. I wasn't looking for it to go. I thought I was doing fine!

Was that after you met Balsekar?

No, no, that was a year and half before. I wasn't interested in Ramesh! *(laughs)* I was interested in getting the shakes stopped enough to get into the car, to get down to the bar for lunch. That was what I was concerned with. And that was my primary concern. My only substantial concern.

I wasn't interested in spiritual matters. I wasn't turning to the guy next to me at the bar and asking, "What do you think is the Source and Substance of everything?" *(laughter)*

So how do you explain what happened?

I don't! Except to say that that was part of the functioning of Totality. That was part of What Is.

When that obsession left, was that Grace?

Absolutely! But my problem was that at that point I considered myself to be the doer. Absolutely, positively, unequivocally, the doer! My whole conditioning was that anything I set my mind to do, I could do. That it was entirely up to me to try a little bit harder, be a little bit smarter, a little slicker, a little quicker, and I could get that which was rightfully mine...more! *(laughs)* And so when this sobriety happened, it was, "Wait a minute! What did this to me?" There's no way in hell I could pretend that I had done it. It was so dramatic. It was so clear. It so boldly...happened...utterly outside of my control or desire, that I could not help but acknowledge the fact that something other than me had done this. I didn't know what. But that was the point at which, Ramana Maharshi would say, my head went into the tiger's mouth, the jaws closed, there was no escape, I was a seeker. At that instant I became a seeker. Because I wanted to know what it was in the universe, that could do this to *me!*

And so I picked up the Tao Te Ching, I started reading Rajneesh and Thich Nat Hahn, and started doing T'ai Chi, and started, you know, breathing through my nose and sitting like so, (which I'd never had the slightest interest in doing before), and I'm doing all that stuff! I'm going to hear Ram Dass talk, and that gets me on a mailing list that gets picked up by the guy who's bringing Ramesh to Los Angeles. And then a flyer comes in the mail saying there's a Guru from India coming. And because I had been at this now for fifteen months, wandering around in the spiritual bazaar, sampling all of these wares, picking up this beautiful shimmery piece over here, and that one over there...and checking this out, and this and that...and having a grand time...I thought, "Well shit! Let's go! It's only a buck! *(laughs)* What have I got to lose?!" And so I went.

So did the enlightenment happen the first time you met him?

No. It was another year and a half.

You were saying that your history of alcoholism and drugs was a preliminary...it broke down the ego and served as a preliminary understanding for the Ultimate Understanding. Do you think that a preliminary understanding usually precedes the Ultimate Understanding?

The preliminary understanding is the point at which one becomes a seeker. In the case of my particular history, I was literally struck sober one night after nineteen years of living a certain way. A profound change took place. And in that instant in which that profound change took place, I could no longer maintain the illusion that I was the one who was doing all of this. I clearly had not done that. So that set me 'on the path.' That was the event that moved this particular body-mind mechanism from living one way to living another, and towards seeking my True Nature. It was the apparent cause for me trying to find out what was the operating principle in the universe, if it wasn't me. If something else was doing this to me, what was it? And so I started reading. Turns out there was ample literature on the subject! I started delving into it, and went through as much as I could go through in the sixteen months before I met Ramesh.

Once on the path...once you become a seeker, consciously, from that point on, are there certain necessary steps before the Ultimate Experience?

There may be a number of experiences that come about. Call them 'free samples' if you will.

Is that customary?

It seems to happen a lot. Have you had any good ones lately?

It's been a while.

They keep you going, don't they? *(laughter)* But no, there are no absolute prerequisites for Awakening.

♋   ♋   ♋

THE SEEKER IS THE ULTIMATE PIG

Could you talk about the origin of the seeking?

Well, all I would say is that the seeking *does* start in certain body-mind mechanisms—in relatively few, actually. Most people simply are not interested. And I would say that of those that seek, virtually all, at one point or another, experience that which they are seeking.

For a short time.

Yes. There is fulfillment of the seeking, in the moment. In other words, there is an experience of that which is sought. This is what I would characterize as the 'top of the pendulum' experience.

Yet most people aren't seeking?

Most people aren't seeking an experience of spiritual oneness, an experience of unity.

The lucky ones.

Yes. That's why the term miserable seeker...(loud laughter)

Guilty as charged!

Because that seeking is for something that can never be attained. There is no permanent *experience* of oneness. The experience of oneness carries with it the seed of the experience of twoness and thus is always temporary.

What is twoness?

It's a city in Northern Africa. *(loud laughter)*

The Transcendence that happens, that is SAID to happen is truly not experiential. It is not the same as the experience of oneness that is experienced with the mystical experience. That's why I make a distinction in this example, between the top of the pendulum experience, and the identification as the fulcrum; and how at the fulcrum there is NOTHING HAPPENING. There is no *experience* of fulcrum-ness, if you will. There is no *experience* of Oneness. The experience of oneness is *always* a dualistic experience. By nature, by definition, experience requires duality. In order to *experience* something, there has to be a subject, and there has to be an object. In the eternal Subjectivity, which is what we all are, when the identification is as the eternal Subject, there is no object to be aware of. All is Subject. All *is* Oneness. And that's why this 'Experience of Awakening,' is often likened to the deep sleep state. Now, very few seekers are seeking the deep sleep state.

They might be seeking to escape the pain of duality.

Right. If seeking an escape from pain, certainly.

And that's what one would expect the search to remove permanently.

Yes. But if that is all you're seeking, then there are ways to obtain oblivion. There's suicide. There's getting hit on the head with a blunt instrument, so that you lose consciousness. There are various drugs that will induce that state. You use them and there is oblivion—there is no longer any pain, or anything else. What the seeker is seeking is permanent PLEASURE! The seeker is the ultimate PIG! The seeker wants it ALL!

Or, as Ram Tzu would say ...

Ram Tzu hears it all the time...

You had a profound, revealing,
Deeply moving spiritual experience.
Now you're hooked.
Now you want more.
Now you are a seeker.

No junkie has ever
Been more dedicated
Or more continually disappointed
Or more miserable.

Once you might
Have been satisfied
With a new car
Or a loving mate.

Now you will settle
For nothing less
Than union with God. *(Loud laughter)*

Ram Tzu knows this ...
You're fucked. *(Laughter)*

There are no one sided coins. There are no single ended sticks. They don't exist. The state of eternal bliss, as an experiential state, does not exist.

Well, that's a relief!

It *is* a relief! When that is deeply and intuitively felt, it is a tremendous relief. That is the relief that comes from the end of the seeking, in the acceptance of WHAT IS. THIS, *(slaps thigh with back of hand)* is What Is, in all its Glory, and all its form.

I'm not a Biblical scholar by any means, but the phrase, "Be still and know that I am God," comes to mind. Be still and know that THIS is God. It isn't out there. It isn't a state to be attained. It IS This.

This is it.

This IS it.

This is what we've all been looking for.

Yes! And this Awakening is an awakening into *this*...the direct experience of *this*, because all of these body-mind mechanisms are instruments of perception! They have senses. They perceive. They experience. The mind in each one of these mechanisms is an instrument of perception, an instrument of experience. And all are animated by Consciousness.

This sense of personal doership...I can see that there is no basis to it. There is no personal doer. But the feeling of personal doership still annoyingly persists. It comes and goes and...

It's only annoying if you don't want it to be there! *(roars with laughter)* And with it, the expectation that if it's not there, THEN the Universe will unfold before you, is a very seductive notion, but it is the notion of the seeker.

So this is what Ramesh is talking about—the identical consciousness of the witness and the non-witness just interplaying simultaneously.

Yes. Yes!

As long as there is the feeling of personal doership the search will go on?

It may.

Yes. It's a part of Totality, and the search will only stop if the feeling of personal doership is gone.

Actually, the seeking can stop just as it started. There are lots of people with a sense of personal doership who don't seek—most people, in fact.

They seek other things. They are also seeking.

Ye-es. But when we talk about seeking we're talking specifically about spiritual seeking, about seeking God, seeking union with the Infinite, that kind of seeking, as opposed to seeking a new car, or a mate, or...

Is not God seeking? Is God not seeking Himself, playing? In that sense everything is seeking; because a tree grows, is growing, seeking.

Well, if you say that every movement is a seeking, certainly. Every movement in this phenomenal manifestation, if you expand your definition, you can certainly say, is a form of seeking. But such expansion sucks the life out of the term.

It is an appealing notion, that God is seeking Himself, because it gives a purpose to this incredible manifestation that is comprehensible to the human mind, "Ah!, this is God setting in motion a process whereby there is disidentification seeking reunification." Such a concept is an overlay on this existence which is as valid as any. But understand that it is a *human mental construct* that is overlaying this phenomenal Reality.

When you came in you started by looking around at everyone in here, everything was still, and it felt like a blessing. There was a feeling that there is nothing that I must do. In that sense, a dog running along just doing his business is enjoying life.

Yes. Yes. And if you *can* accept life like a dog does, by all means, do! *(Roars with laughter).* As much as is possible! And understand also that there are times when you will not enjoy or accept life. Life will not be enjoyable.

∽

Regarding seeking and the sense of personal doership; you said just before that there are lots of people with a sense of personal doership who don't seek. But once you have become a seeker, is it usually true that as long as there is a sense of personal doership there will be seeking?

Yes, but not necessarily so. Certainly, in the absence of personal doership, there is no seeking. But the seeking can also fall away prior to the falling away of a sense of personal doership. The seeking can arise and just as suddenly stop. And it can stop, and in fact it frequently *does* stop, precedent to the sense of personal doership falling away.

For me, essentially that's what happened. I hung around Ramesh, I published his books, I edited his books, I understood the teaching. I mean, this is not rocket science. This is pretty basic, a fundamentally easy teaching to understand. "All there is, is Consciousness, Consciousness is all there is." How difficult is that? So I got that. I really bought the whole package and said, "If that's true then it's all unfolding *just* the way it's supposed to, and I'm doing what I'm supposed to. And if I'm supposed to, I seek, if I'm not supposed to seek I won't seek. It's just happening." And I relaxed in that. There was a relaxing that happened in that. And that happened *prior* to this final falling away of the sense of personal doership. I was still doing all the same stuff. I was running around with Ramesh and operating my business and all the rest of it, but the seeking, the sense that there was something over *there* that I was going to *get* if I just did this, that or the other thing, was gone. Which was very nice, for me, personally. I enjoyed that. It took a lot of the load off, a lot of the pressure of 'getting' something was gone.

But you stayed with Ramesh, or did you go away?

There was no reason to go away. That's what was happening. My life had become entwined with his, at a number of different levels, so that relationship continued. And later after this sense of personal doership fell away, I continued to be with him whenever I could, and I'm off to Bombay again in two months. And I promise you, the *only reason* that I would go to India is because Ramesh is there. There is *no other* reason for me to go to Bombay. I do not like Bombay. At all. *(laughter)* And when he's gone I will never set foot in India again.......... maybe. *(long loud laughter)*

♋   ♋   ♋

Man was predestined to have free will.
Hal Lee Luyah

Ram Tzu knows this:
Your choices are like votes
In a one party political system.

Everyone is driving from the back seat.
Wayne

The pursuit of mastery
Over yourself
Is as worthwhile
As gaining control of
Your shadow.

You approach your life
As you would a chess game.
You want to win so you
Consider each move
Mentally playing out every permutation.

Ram Tzu knows this:
Life is not confined by 64 squares.
And God your opponent,
Keeps changing the rules.

Call it a dream. It does not change anything.
Ludwig Wittgenstein

FOUR

THE SENSE OF PERSONAL DOERSHIP

NAVIGATING YOUR BOAT ACROSS THE SEAS OF SAMSARA

Can you talk a little bit about personal will?

Personal will? If you can show me it, I can talk about it. What do you mean by personal will?

Making good choices, bad choices. Making a choice.

So where does the will part come in the making of this choice?

I don't know if I am correct in thinking this, but I think that you think it is guided by Consciousness.

Not guided actually but entirely done by. Now, I'm from Los Angeles. In Los Angeles we have, among other things, Disneyland. And at Disneyland they have a wonderful ride called the Motorboat Ride. I don't know how many of you have been to Disneyland and have availed yourselves of the Motorboat Ride. For those of you who haven't, I'll describe it for you. You stand in line for two hours...*(laughter)* At the end of the two hours you come out onto a dock, and a motorboat pulls up with a bench seat which seats four people across. The four of you get on and the boat takes off, and everybody has a Captain's wheel. Everybody gets to drive the boat.

So, the boat takes off and, of course, you're a diligent boat-driver, and you see that the watercourse up ahead curves to the right, so you turn your wheel to the right. And the boat goes to the right, and you experience a tremendous sense of satisfaction at the grand way you are driving the boat. Now the watercourse turns to the left, you turn your wheel to the left, the boat goes to the left. Very satisfying. Then the watercourse forks. And you decide to take the boat to the right. You turn your wheel to the right and the boat goes to the left.

You've got a problem here! You were doing so well. You were driving the boat so excellently, and now you must have screwed up somehow. The reasonable thing to assume is that you've made some kind of ghastly error, and *if* you can just hone your boat driving skills, you can get the boat to go in the direction you want. So, you take a boat-driving seminar. *(laughter)* We have lots of those in Los Angeles. There are pages and pages in the newspaper, promising that in five, ten, fifteen, twenty, simple short courses, they will help you get control of your boat, such that you can get it to go *exactly* where you want it to go.

So, you plunk down your money, and you take the boat-driving seminar, and at the end of the boat-driving seminar you get back in the boat and you turn the wheel to the right and the boat goes to the right. You say, "That was an excellent seminar," and you recommend it to all your friends. You say, "It has done wonders for my boat driving skills. I'm able to turn the wheel to the right and the boat goes to the right, turn the wheel to the left and the boat goes to the left, everything's great." But when you come to the fork in the waterway and turn the wheel to the right, the boat goes to the left. So you think, "I must have forgotten something fundamental that they taught me in the course, because it was working so well before!"

So, you sign up for the refresher course—and they do offer a refresher course because you're not the first person to have experienced this particular problem. At the end of the refresher course you get in the boat and turn your wheel to the right and the boat goes to the right, you turn your wheel to the left and the boat goes to the left, you come to the fork in the waterway, you turn your wheel to the right and the boat goes to the left again. And your natural conclusion is that the course was actually not so good after all. You might even be tempted to give up on all such courses. Just then your friend calls and says, "I know the course we took was really lousy and didn't really teach us how to control the boat, but I just found *another* course and this one works! I turned my wheel to the right and my boat went to the right, and I turned my wheel to the left and the boat went to the left..." And if you are a seeker, IF YOU ARE A SEEKER, you will go!

Now, is it not extraordinary, that through this whole process, it never occurs to you, the thought never enters your mind that this wheel isn't connected to anything? *(laughter)* Despite all the evidence to the contrary! You look at your life, all of your intentions, all of the times that you were *absolutely* certain of what it was that you wanted to do! And then you worked so hard and diligently to do them. And your life went *that way*. Time and time again, your best efforts did not yield the desired results. And yet you say "I'm the master of my destiny. I choose what I want to do." But your wheel isn't connected to anything! And yet you don't see it! How is that possible? And that's why Ramesh's description of this as the Divine Hypnosis is really so wonderful.

ᏹ   ᏹ   ᏹ

WHAT IS DIVINE HYPNOSIS?

What is divine hypnosis?

The hypnosis which enables this entire play to look the way it does. It is this sense of personal doership, that exists in virtually every body-mind mechanism, which, in large measure, shapes the way that this "play" plays out. That sense of personal doership is integral to the response of these mechanisms.

How does it come about?

Okay, this is where I get to do my Kleenex trick. No rabbits, though. *(laughter)* Sai Baba materializes jewelry; I do tissues.

(A balled up tissue appears in Wayne's hand) If we think of this as Consciousness, All There Is—It has no quality, no characteristic, just pure Isness, pure Potentiality—at some point, because It is alive. It is not deadness, there is vitality to It. It expresses, and that vitality manifests. Physicists call it The Big Bang, clerics call it Genesis, the point at which the phenomenal universe comes into being. And the way we can describe it is that out of this

undifferentiated Consciousness comes the physical manifestation of universes.

(*Wayne pulls tendrils out from the balled tissue*) These universes are 'expressed' or 'extruded' out of that Potentiality, and out of this little universe there comes a solar system (pulls tendrils out of tendrils) and out of that solar system there comes a planet, and out of that planet is extruded an individual human organism. Now mind you, this is all connected. At no point has anything become separate. This is all One. This, (*tearing off a small corner of the tissue*) never happens at any time, because Consciousness is all there is, that's all there ever has been, that's all there ever will be. So, every *thing* is an expression—an extrusion, if you will—of this Consciousness. Nothing is separate. Thus, you have an individual who is born, lives a certain span of years, or days, or weeks, or months, and then returns back into the Whole. It can't go anywhere else, because this is all there is. Each of the so-called individuals who consider themselves to be separate are in fact not separate. There *is* no separation, there is only Oneness. But for this universe to *be,* there has to be the *appearance* of separateness. And that appearance of separateness arises at the moment of the 'conception' of the universe, as part of the arising of the phenomenal universe.

There must be some agency through which this universe can be perceived. Perception is crucial. Without some means of perceiving, then there is what there has always been: Consciousness. What gives Consciousness characteristics, what gives all these extrusions qualities, is something to perceive them. And the nature of these qualities is a function of the nature of what is perceiving. And crucial to this manifestation being as it appears to us now is this sense that we are individual doers. That's what Ramesh calls the Divine Hypnosis. And one of the

qualities of hypnosis is that it changes your 'reality' by
virtue of the way that you perceive it.

So if you're given a hypnotic suggestion that your
clothes are on fire, you will have that subjective experience. The 'reality' of the situation will be that your clothing
is on fire. You may go to a guru and ask for help. You ask
him to put the fire out. And he will tell you that there is
no fire there. Well, this is not what you want to hear.
You say, "Hey, I'm burning up here, help me. Don't just
give me philosophy!" Now at this point all sorts of things
may happen. He may give you a mantra to distract you
or prescribe various other practices or he may continue
to point out that the fire is truly not there. But no matter
what he says, no matter what you do, there never has
been a fire there. So, when the hypnotic suggestion is
removed, what happens to the fire?

You think that you are the doer, and therefore you
respond according to that belief. You cannot do otherwise until such time as that belief is removed. So, it's all
God, it's all Totality, it's all Consciousness, it's all One.
And yet there is the *appearance* of the many, because we
don't see the connection.

But this is not some limitation on your part. It is not
some shortcoming that has to be overcome, but rather
an aspect of your basic nature. And the same Force that
put it there, the same Hypnotist, must also then be re-
sponsible for removing it.

♋   ♋   ♋

HOW CAN THE DIVINE
HYPNOSIS BE REMOVED ?

So it can only happen when the Divine enters your body-mind and decides to dissolve the sense of personal doership because you can't do it yourself?

The Divine has never *not* been in your body-mind. Your body-mind *is* the Divine. It has no need to enter anywhere. It is never NOT there.

The idea of the personal doer obscures the knowledge of that though.

Yes.

And it can't undo itself?

It cannot. Any more than a shadow can move on its own.

So it has to be an outside agent that creates the transition?

You can call it an outside agent. The reason it cannot undo itself is because it has no substance, no independent substance. It is powerless. The only power it has is that of Totality. It is Totality's power. It is Totality's functioning, whether the body-mind mechanism knows it or not.

The thing that seems to be there that keeps the Awakening from occurring is the fear that seems to arise from nowhere, because the dream-self does not want to be annihilated. It wants to hang around, apparently.

But even then whose fear is it? Is it not even then Totality's fear, functioning through that particular body-mind mechanism?

Doesn't seem like a very elegant way to operate the universe.

On the contrary! *(laughter)* It's supremely elegant. It is only inelegant from the standpoint of the individual who says, "I just want good stuff. There shouldn't be any bad stuff. Or if there must be bad stuff, have somebody else get that, and I'll take the good stuff. I'll be the saint, somebody else can be the sinner. Somebody else can be the murderer. I'll be the Nobel Laureate."

♋   ♋   ♋

WHAT ABOUT PERSONAL RESPONSIBILITY?

Well isn't that the way it appears to be when you compare Mother Teresa and Hitler?

What's that?

That one is being the saint, and one is not?

Exactly. But if you have a choice, who the hell wants to be the reviled, hated, spat-upon murderer or child molester? I mean, Hitler at least got some good press from a lot of people. How about the child-molester, the one whom *nobody* likes? The one who is compelled to commit the horror. If you have the choice, do you choose to be that? Or do you choose to be the one whom everyone loves, whom everyone adores? Who gets bouquets at their feet.

So no one would choose to be the reviled, horrific one.

No. In fact, Ram Tzu wrote a poem about that:

Ram Tzu has a question for you...

You are kind to others.
You give to charity.
You go to church.
You pray with sincerity.
You are honest in your business.
You fulfill your obligations.
You know yourself to be a good man.

Where did all those qualities come from?
How is it that your heart is not swollen
With the rage and despair
That causes a man
To slaughter his own children?
Are you really so different from him?

Follow the spoor of your blessings
To their source.
There will be God.

You know, I actually see components of both men in myself. But I wasn't clear about follow the spoor of your blessings, because that implies that the things that you value as being good are your blessings. Maybe those murderous feelings are your blessings too if they lead you to finding the Source.

One of the nice things about being a poet is you can say shit like that. *(laughter)* The fact is, that yes, if you follow the spoor of either, of any of your qualities to their source, there you will find the Source! But it's more poetic the way I wrote it. *(laughter)*

But then you're saying that the person that murders his children, if he's diligent about following that course, may be an enlightened man?

Not through his diligence, but Awakening can theoretically happen anywhere, anytime. Absolutely.

Because there are no enlightened men. You see? It is an impersonal happening.

I always find that a little bit disturbing that every-thing is one Totality, and the guy that does get that rage and goes out and murders his children—it troubles me. What sort of Totality is this for something like that to happen?

A very *whole* one.

This doesn't make me feel any better about it.

It wasn't designed to. You want to feel better, go to a temple or a church. They'll tell you, God is Love, God is Good, God is Kindness, God is everything wonderful. And as long as you don't ask any disturbing questions like, "Well, if God is all these things and is all powerful, then how do you explain all this crap going on?" And they say, "Well, there's the Devil and er-er-er." It gets real messy, because then God must not be all powerful and then it's not God and there's not a Oneness, it's now a Twoness, *and* if there's a Twoness, how does the...?" And it just goes on.

What we're talking about here is What Is, not how *you* think it should be, how *you* would like it to be, how *you*, if you were God, would make it! God is not human-hearted. We would all say that if you could discover the cure for the AIDS virus it would be a great thing. You would be *canonized*, you would be given the Nobel Prize, everybody would love you, you would make a gazillion dollars, everything would be terrific. From the standpoint of you and the rest of the world, a great thing will have happened. But from the standpoint of the AIDS virus, you're a genocidal maniac! *(Loud laughter)* You will have *wiped out* an entire life form. You would be deemed worse than Hitler.

If it all is supposed to happen the way it is, then what about social action?

You see, your reactions are supposed to happen the way they are too. Social actions are quite obviously also part of What Is. If this body-mind mechanism is programmed in such a way that it reacts to suffering with some kind of action to alleviate, or attempt to alleviate the suffering in somebody else, that is what will happen. The actions that happen through the body-mind mechanism happen as part of the functioning of Totality, not as part of your decision that if you are in a particular situation you will decide to act 'this way.' The same principle is in effect regardless of whether there is a sense of personal doership there or not. It is the same Consciousness acting through the body-mind mechanism that we call a sage that creates action, in accordance with the programmed characteristics of that body-mind mechanism.

♋   ♋   ♋

WHOSE KARMA?

What about Karma?

Karma simply is cause and effect. There is within this phenomenal manifestation the appearance of cause and effect. And karma describes this relationship between events. One thing causes another. The question more importantly is, "Who is doing the action?" That is, if we step back to the root cause of the action then we ask, "Whose Karma is it?" If Consciousness is what is functioning, if it is Consciousness that is operating through all of these mechanisms then it is Consciousness' karma. There's no question that our minds create cause and effect relationship between things, and that there is the appearance of a progression through the phenomenal manifestation — things progress, there are advancements in science and music and all of these require new body-mind mechanisms to be created to advance the storyline.

Thus, if we understand that the karma is happening through these various body-mind mechanisms, terrific! There's no problem. It is only a problem when we get into the question of personal doership, suggesting that any of these body-mind mechanisms has any individual say in their actions. If they did, all of these Buddhist countries in which there is a belief in karma, in which you are going to be rewarded or punished in your future life, would be kind, generous places where everybody would be helping everybody else. Of course everyone would do that! Wouldn't they? To gain merit in the next life—they'd have to be nuts not to. The whole misunderstanding about 'personal' karma revolves around the notion that there is a separate 'you' who is the doer. Once it is understood that Consciousness is the doer then the whole question of 'personal' karma becomes moot.

ᗃ   ᗃ   ᗃ

GRACE

As I look back on my life, I feel like the moments of Grace were certainly nothing that I accomplished.

Well that conclusion is almost inescapable when you do look. Anyone who examines their life, and the events— the really important crucial ones—can see that they almost all come out of left field, completely unexpected, unrehearsed, unprepared-for. One day you're going along in this direction, and the next day you're over here, through no intention of your own. And I think that that's pretty much everybody's experience. In fact I'm sure it is. Now whether you can recognize that or not, is another matter. But if you say that you have clearly examined your life and identified the fact that over the course of time, all of these things have happened rather than you're doing them, then that's a start. Now the question is why do you forget that? Why isn't it your experience in the moment that God, or Totality, or Consciousness, or whatever, is running the show? Why do you think that it is incumbent upon you to make certain decisions, and do this or that, and concern yourself with, "Should I do this, or should I do that?" If, in fact, the recognition is that you're not doing it, why do you still *feel* like you're doing it?

Are you asking me?

Yes!

Well the image I have is that I try to ride the fence. I try to live in two worlds. There's a worldly aspect that feels divided from my God self, and all the attractions, all the isms, all the schisms just pull me out. And I stop staying sacred, stop knowing I'm sacred.

So, you have this incredible peace, oneness, unity, on this one side, which is marvelous...absolute peace. And then you've got the chaos and all of this suffering on the other side, and you say, "I'm choosing to straddle this fence." Why would you choose to straddle the fence, if you had the choice to just throw a leg over and hop into the peace?

Well...I don't know.

Exactly. I mean, there's certainly various ways to approach it. But the image that my Guru, Ramesh, suggested is that the reason that we don't do that, is because we can't. Because we are not the doers, even in that! This sense of personal doership that is there, that is unmistakable, that exists, that is as real as you are, is what he calls the Divine Hypnosis. This is what has been given to you as part of this whole dance of life and living, to make the dance of life and living look the way it does.

I like that.

I liked it too. Whenever you have the notion of doership, no matter how subtle and spiritual it gets—and it can get pretty subtle—as soon as it is said, "You can't do anything *except* be earnest. You can't do anything *except* inquire into your own true nature," as soon as there's an "except," and you don't do that thing, you're a fuck-up again! And it becomes your fault, one more time, that you're not enlightened, that you're not at peace all the time, that you're not in the absolute perfect harmony with What Is. And that's why when there is this sense of, "Yes, everything, without exception, is precisely as it should be, that these human bodies are all instruments through which God or Totality is functioning perfectly," there can be tremendous peace. And you say, "Pheeewww. Yeah."

Now where that gets tricky is what about the child molester? What about the rapist? What about Hitler? It's all well and good that God makes sunsets and puppies *(laughs)* but what about all the crap? The stuff you don't like. The stuff that hurts your heart. What about that stuff? Is that perfect? And it doesn't even have to be Hitler, how about those characteristics in you that cause harm to others? How about the fact that despite your best efforts, you still keep hurting people? When there's the understanding that this manifestation is the perfect functioning of God, or Consciousness, or Totality, in that acceptance is peace. And yet, that acceptance can only happen. You can't *will* the acceptance to happen. It can only happen. And when it does, we call it Grace.

You can say it's the Grace of God, that you are centered, you are at one, you are at peace, you are in harmony, you have acceptance of What Is. Acceptance doesn't mean you necessarily like it. Acceptance doesn't mean you approve of it. Acceptance doesn't mean that you're not going to act in the next moment to change it. It means there is acceptance that in this moment, it is What Is. Acceptance of What Is is peace.

♋   ♋   ♋

LIMITED FREE WILL?

Can there not be a subtle interaction with the Eternal...

You mean, like *limited* free will? *(laughter)*

Why not?

Why not? Because if it's limited it's not free!

What about the idea that you don't really have control but you can direct your intentions?

What's the difference? Doesn't it just piss you off? It always pisses me off when someone says, "You can't do anything, you have no power, you are a puppet but, you *can* do this." You either can or you can't! You are either an instrument through which Totality is functioning, therefore the actions are Totality's actions, or you aren't. It is one or the other. Limited free will!! Am I the only one who doesn't get that? If it is limited where is the freedom?

I just feel that if I don't direct my intentions that somehow everything will fall apart.

That is very common. That is what the ego says: "If I'm not in charge the whole thing is going to go down the tubes!" Look at your experience, look at your life, all the times you said I'm going to go there and your life ends up over here. Everybody, it is not just you, everybody. Look at your life, all your intentions. You set out to go there, how come you keep ending up over here? Is it because you're not intentioning well enough? That is what the mind says. That is what the ego says. That is what the sense of personal doership says, "I'm not doing it well enough, if I could just get control of this thing, if I could just do it well enough then I could make this work. I could get what I want!"

If I just had clearer intentions...

"If I *just*, if I *just* did this, if I *just* didn't do that." Yes! That is what this sense of personal doership says, which Ramesh describes as the Divine Hypnosis. This sense of personal doership is like a hypnosis in which the experience is that I am doing it! The belief continues that I am doing it and you ignore all the evidence to the contrary. You don't see it, you are literally hypnotized into not seeing that your steering wheel is not connected. This is not your fault. You did not hypnotize yourself. This happened as part of the conditioning of this body-mind mechanism at about age two and a half. It happens to virtually all humans and most go through life without ever questioning this.

I can take your argument so far, that I'm not in control of certain things. But EVERYTHING—no!

Do you know what Nisargadatta Maharaj said when someone said to him what you just said to me?

No.

He said, "You can't accept it? Fine, then suffer!"

But I chose to put my hand up to ask this question.

Yes, you say, "This is my choice. I am deciding to put my hand up." But is not the decision, the ability to put your hand up when you decide to, a function of your nature? In other words, there are people in this room who are so shy, that even when they want to put their hand up, can't put their hand up.

There's a limitation in their nature, in their program, which prohibits them from doing that which they want to do! Your body-mind mechanism doesn't have that inhibition. Not because it chose not to have that inhibition, but because its programming, its basic fundamental nature combined with its subsequent conditioning, has brought it to a point today where it is capable of making the movement from the thought, "I want to put my hand up," to being able to put its hand up!

Therefore, the ability to, 'make that choice' is given. It is conditioned by your nature.

Yeah? But within those limitations, there's choice.

That is like saying a prisoner in jail is actually 'free' because he is 'free' to move from his bed to the toilet. There is the *appearance* of choice, yes. You say, "I apparently am choosing to do that." But your choice is conditioned by your nature. Now, your nature *changes*, moment to moment, so what you choose to do in this moment, you might very well *not* choose to do in the next. The nature of the organism changes moment to moment as a result of various outside influences, or even inside influences such as hormonal changes and blood sugar changes. Having a horrible thought, might throw you into depression such that you can't bear to even be recognized by another human being, much less ask a question of one. All of that can happen within the span of a couple of seconds! And how you 'choose' to act will be very different depending on your state of mind.

Okay. (laughter) That's possible. Well, I don't know if that's possible. You know, it's not apparent to me if it's happening like that.

That is the point. This is what we are talking about— this Divine Hypnosis. There is an overlay on these actions, which is deep and profound, and it says, "These are *my* actions," and even people who are more agreeable than you, will say, "Yeah, Wayne's right—what he says is absolutely the Truth. I believe him completely, because he agrees with what I think." *(laughter)* Those people who say, "This is the Truth, that in fact you have no choice, it is all the will of Consciousness, Consciousness is in charge, all there is is Consciousness, Consciousness is functioning"—even for these people, as long as there's a sense of personal doership, they still have the subjective experience that, "I'm doing it."

♋   ♋   ♋

A HIGHER SELF?

Do you believe in the concept of a Higher Self?

Of a Higher Self? I don't know what that is.

But you said you'd been involved with spiritual teachings.

I probably wasn't paying attention when they were teaching the Higher Self. *(laughter)*

The idea that there's a spiritual power making you have certain choices, leading you.

Who is this 'You' that is being led?

Well the self, the...

The small self? The individual ...

The tiny, tiny little self.

Well, if we can locate what that is, and if that exists independent of the greater Self, then we might be able to see the relationship between them. I see a continuity between them. I don't see any difference between this Higher Self and this small self.

The idea is that you're not always connected to this Higher Self.

You can't be disconnected from It. All there is, is It. *(laughter)* That's all there is! *(roars with laughter)* Consciousness is all there is. The Higher Self is all there is. It expresses through all of these body-mind mechanisms which we call the little self.

I'm not constantly in tune with that. It's only at times that I can tune into that. Therefore, at times that I'm not tuned into the Higher Self, I have to make decisions for this tiny little being.

Yes, you must make those decisions. Those decisions *must* be made.

What I'm maintaining is, that it's not constantly coming through me to make me act in a certain way, but it can operate through me sometimes.

And what I'm suggesting is that it *is* operating through you at *all* times, whether you can feel the connection with it or not: that even your feeling of disconnection is It!

☞   ☞   ☞

GOD'S WILL

Could the mind-body do the legwork and do the wrong leg-work?

I understand your question, and it's a good one. I mean basically you're asking: Does a particular body-mind mechanism have any influence at all; can *it* decide of its own free will, of its own volition, whether to do something or not to do something and thus sin?

Right.

That's what we're talking about. Can it, *on its own*, do *other* than God's Will?

There are times when there is that question, "Am I doing the right thing?" You feel like you have some kind of control there, and you don't want to make the wrong decision. Am I doing God's will or am I...?

Absolutely. Yes, that feeling arises, because the subjective sense within the body-mind mechanism is that I *do* have choice. I *do* have volition. Now Ram Tzu would have something to say about that:

> You think there's something wrong
> There must have been a mistake
> You think things should be different
> By different you mean better
> And you're pretty sure
> You know what better is.
>
> You would eliminate
> All the bad stuff:
>
> War
> Disease
> Suffering
> Famine
> Pollution.

Would be good for starters.
Who could argue with that?

You would save cute animals
You would ban bombs
You would halt injustice
You would make everyone happy.

Why not?
It could happen.

And if it does, Ram Tzu knows this...
God will be grateful
For your help.

Every one of these body-mind mechanisms is an *instrument* through which Totality functions. It is this Totality that is operative. It is this Consciousness that infuses these body-mind mechanisms. It is Consciousness that is making the choice. It is Consciousness that has *designed* each of these body-mind mechanisms in such a way that its *natural* reaction, *in the moment,* is to choose in a certain way. And because that body-mind mechanism has been given this sense of personal doership, it says, "*I'm* choosing." But the choice is a function of the *nature* of the organism.

So between the stimulus and its response, if there is this place to choose, and it looks like a choice, is it really not a choice?

It is really not a choice by 'you.' The choice is being made by a *million, billion* influences over which *you* have no control. And how you choose, how you will react will differ from second to second because your conditioning changes from instant to instant. The hormonal balances in your body shift instant to instant. The psychological attitude shifts instant to instant. Some thought comes through your mind—all of a sudden a memory comes, and your whole attitude changes. As a result, the way you react one second is different from the way you would react the next second. Now you don't have any *control* over the arising of these thoughts that come into your mind totally unbidden—they arise. The reaction of the mechanism to the thought is also an automatic response. So the organism, when it is faced with a stimulus, will react in the moment and then say, "Well that's how I reacted. That's what I chose to do."

Now I would put to you, if you could make the choice, if you could choose, would you have chosen to have a life like this? Couldn't you have done better than this? *(laughter)*

♋   ♋   ♋

WHY THE DUALISM?

In Ram Tzu's poem, the statement that, "God would appreciate your help," seems like the essence of dualism. In other words, we're running around here thinking that we're doing something and God's doing something else. Can you discuss the theory about why Consciousness would dispense this dualistic theory so liberally among everyone?

So that *this* life and living, as it is now, could happen. Without the dualistic perception—without the sense of personal doership—*this* does not happen. Something else happens. And at this instant, this *is!* However you want to characterize it (whether you want to characterize it as a dream, or whether you want to characterize it as an alternate universe) I don't care how you characterize it, but *here it is.* And part and parcel of this is the sense of personal doership.

Whenever you're asking *why*, you are looking for an explanation that will make sense within your particular mental structure, within your sensibility of how this universe is. You want to fit it in. To the question, "Why?" Ramesh uses an example to point to this. I've told this before but it bears repeating. You take kids to the beach. You give them a bucket and some shovels and set them loose for a couple of hours, and what do they do? They build a sandcastle. And they'll expend a lot of effort building towers and moats and tunnels, and all kinds of great stuff. Then at the end of the two hours, you say, "Alright kids, it's time to go." And what do they do? They jump on it. They kick it. They moosh it back down into nothing. And you say, *"Why* did you do that? Can you tell me why you did that? You spent all that time creating this thing, and then in an instant you destroyed it." And they'll look at you like you're crazy: "What do you mean *why?" (laughter)* "It's what we *did!"* And if you really press them, they'll say, "Well, it was *fun!"* But their understanding is that that's just what was happening. You see? There was no intention or objective.

The adult human mind wants to make sense of things by drawing a box around events, so that it can then relate the events within this narrow framework and create a world-view. And so anything that comes into that space the mind tries to relate to everything else, and if it can do it successfully there is a comfortable worldview. If it can't, things get a little messy, a little uncomfortable. It has to expand the box (maybe) a little bit, to expand the worldview.

But what we're talking about here is the action of *God!* God (being everything) is too big to draw a box around. You can't circumscribe this Totality with any mental structure to make sense of it. Totality does not operate from an adult human perspective.

So, any question about *why* is a natural enough one to arise. It certainly does, and has for millennia. And religions are in the business of answering 'why' questions. So you can have quite elaborate discussions about why things are the way they are. And there are beautiful stories of original sin, and being cast out of the garden, and all of these kinds of explanations as to why there's evil. And what I suggest is if you really, really want an answer, scan the literature, find one that satisfies you, and adopt it, for as long as it's comforting. There are a million of them. There are all kinds of answers. Pick one! But the underlying understanding is that this is What *Is*.

♋   ♋   ♋

IF NOT DOERSHIP, WHAT ABOUT CHOICE?

I happen to believe that we all make choices throughout the day, but whether some people would be free to make that choice or not could be another matter.

That's absolutely clear. There is a very potent experience of choice. I don't think anybody would deny that there was that. You have a fairly long row to hoe if you're saying that there's no *appearance* of choice, because if there's one thing you will get from everyone in the room, it is confirmation of the fact that there is this sense that "I have to choose. I have to make a decision here in this moment between two things." As long as there is within the body-mind unit the sense that "I'm a doer, I do stuff," then these decisions that get made—that have to be continually made—are experienced as being 'my' decisions. The interesting question is: *is* that, in fact, the case? Are they truly *your* decisions, and are you free to decide however you want to decide?

I agree that ultimately we're not the doer. I don't think I'm the doer, but I think we do have the choice. I find that moment to moment I'm choosing between fear and love.

Fear and love?

Yes. And depending upon which of those is responding within me, it is something that I feel I can really recognize as a wounded aspect of myself. So, if I can sort of deal with that part before responding back, then once I take care of my own woundedness, I may be able to see that the person who did what I believe was an insult to me is just wounded himself, and that can open me up to compassion as opposed to me responding in a more aggressive way.

So is that what you always do, then?

No.

No? Why not?

Because I often act out of my wounded self.

Okay, so if you're saying that you're acting out of your 'wounded self,' then you're saying you don't have control over yourself, that sometimes your wounded-self conditioning exerts itself independent of your will. Your will would, of course, be to choose love rather than fear all of the time, I assume. If you were able to exercise such will unimpeded, you would presumably be a loving person all the time.

I literally deal with it as a muscle. I mean, when we first go into a gym to exercise a muscle, generally we can't lift very heavy weights. I think love is a muscle, and that because of certain things which happen from birth on, it sort of gets atrophied and that it's a matter of me sort of reworking that muscle.

Yes, I would agree with you. I think that clearly, all kinds of things have happened to you since birth which have affected that muscle. People harmed you, people hurt you—maybe in profound ways, maybe in subtle ways. But you didn't have any control over those factors, and those things shaped this particular muscle. So, if those events shaped the muscle such that you can't react in the way that you would ideally like to react, where does this choice or free will come in?

I think that's the choice of the in-going process. I think that if you notice in your life that you're walking around angry all the time, and you're suddenly noticing, "God, I don't have any friends, and isn't it interesting that I really have no intimacies in my life? There's no love in my life." Then you start to take stock of how much negativity you have, and how, let's say, wounded you still are, how angry you still are, and then you start slowly finding ways to heal the parts that are controlling again.

But how is it that you start to see that? You just said, "*If* you notice..." That is a very big *if*. Why is it that your body-mind mechanism starts to notice, while there are thousands of others that are equally wounded, equally damaged, equally pained, that don't see it? It wasn't that one day you willed yourself to start seeing the damage and the unhappiness. It happened. All of a sudden one day there was a new vision. There was a recognition of how negative things were, and then because you are who you are there was the reaction: "Something has to be done about this." Whereas other people will look around, see this pain, see the suffering, see the damage done to them, and kill themselves.

Right.

How is it that your reaction was to start working out to make the love-muscle stronger? *(laughter)*

I guess it's just everybody's own way upon the journey, and I actually think everybody is moving in that direction as a people.

That is a lovely sentiment. I guess you don't read the newspaper.

That's why I think people connect to people through a sort of soul-level, because I think that we as souls do yearn for that light, love, connection, union. There are people here, and then there are people out in horror right now; it's just a different angle of the same struggle.

I agree that it's all part of the same process. It's a process of life and living. There are some people who, for whatever reason, become seekers; who care about healing this split experience between themselves and the world at large. Then there are others who experience the split who don't even recognize that they're experiencing the split. For them there is just an incredible emptiness, and they become either drug addicts or alcoholics or food addicts or meditation addicts or anything that will temporarily heal this wound. So, it's absolutely true that these movements exist within this phenomenal world. Clearly they do. But not everyone is interested in consciously seeking their own true nature. Actually, relatively few people are interested in seeking their true nature. That isn't obvious if most of your friends are seekers. But most people are interested in seeking more money, or a better mate, so that in their sex-relations and their money-relations, they can get more influence or power so that they're not feeling so afflicted by the world, and they can exert their 'will' more. They want power in their job, a promotion, so that instead of being on the bottom of the pile, they can be on the top of the pile. Those are the things that most people are interested in. Believe it or not, when people hear that there's someone in Hermosa Beach talking about the nature of Being, and that it destroys all of your concepts—relatively few people say: "Oh, let's *go* !" *(laughter)*

Are you saying my being here wasn't up to me?

Yes, you have to be here. Right now you have to be here, you could not be anywhere else. People who have to be at the ball game are at the ball game, people who have to be at the opera are at the opera.

Which is not to say that in the next moment you may not change. The thought could readily come in the very next instant, "This sucks...this guy is an idiot." (laughter) "I'm out of here." And then the next thought may be, "Somebody said that new movie was very good, I'll leave here and see if that new movie has started."

We'll just have to see what the next moment brings. But, up to this point, the thought that brought you here you assume was the cause for your being here...how did you find out that this was happening today?

I got a flyer.

Okay. So a flyer came in the mail unbidden, advising you that this event was happening and the thought arose, "I think I'll go do this." Now in order to do this, all kinds of other things had to happen. You not only had to have the desire, you had to have the time. You made the decision to come. How did you get here?

I drove.

You drove a car. So, you got into the car and you turned the key into the ignition and what happened? The car started, I assume? Does that always happen?

No.

So the 5,000 moving parts in the car had to cooperate. You got on the road, how far did you drive?

About seventy miles.

So, in those seventy miles you passed several thousand motorists, passing you at a combined speed of over 100 miles an hour. If any one of them had had even the slightest physical alteration in the body-mind mechanism such that there was a movement of the steering wheel of only 2 degrees...you wouldn't be here. None of those thousands of body-mind mechanisms in those thousands of vehicles did that. None of this was in your control. All of the parts in your car maintained their structural integrity. All the molecules worked. But none of that was in your control. All of that simply happened. All of it enabled you to arrive here and when you got here you say, " I decided to come here." The entire Universe had to cooperate to get you here or you wouldn't be here. Yet you say, "The *reason* I am here is because *I* decided to come."

♋   ♋   ♋

NO FREEDOM OF DECISION?

Then I have no freedom in the decision making process?

If you can show me where the freedom is in the choice, I am game. I am interested. Nothing I say is the Truth, therefore I suggest you not take my word for anything. I would suggest that you listen to what I say and check it out for yourself. Don't trust me. Look at your life. Look at the events and see to what degree you have freedom. See where the choice is and what the nature of that choice is...if you can. *(laughter)*

It feels like it gets murky because it seems more likely that I would arrive here than not, because many of the things that I choose to do transpire. I can see all the reasons why they wouldn't, but there seems to be a seductive pattern.

I agree, so let's look, shall we, at this choice of the decision to come here. The decision to come was made through a body-mind mechanism that was interested in this subject. There were lots of other body-mind mechanisms who received the same information. They got a flyer in the mail. They looked at the flyer and they said "No way!" *(laughing)* Okay, so, how is it that this body-mind mechanism saw the flyer and made the decision to do something. It had to be interested. It had to be a seeker in order for the decision to be made to do it. Non-seekers are not interested in coming to Advaita talks, and I have given enough of them to be able to tell you this. I don't really expect you to take my word for it but...

I can see why they wouldn't.

You can see why they wouldn't? *(laughter)* Excellent! So, that being the case, your choice to come, your decision to come is conditioned by the fact that you are a seeker. Your being a seeker, how did that start? When did you choose to be a seeker?

I don't recall actually choosing it. It just sort of happened.

Okay. You see that the seeking *happened.* The seeking, the impulse arose in you to seek. You didn't one day decide that life was much too calm and peaceful and it was time to become a seeker. So, when the seeking started through no fault of your own or decision of your own, it set into motion this process that culminated with the decision being made (upon receipt of this flyer) to attend the talk. So, if you can show me where in this process is the free, unconditioned will to decide one way or the other, I'm interested.

For 30 years, ever since reading Be Here Now, *there is part of me that believes what you are saying. But I only get it about sixty percent.*

Be Here Now has probably sold a million copies. As Ramesh's publisher I can assure you *(laughing)* that for those books that take the understanding that is there in *Be Here Now* and bring it up the next forty percent, the interest in that additional forty percent is minimal. It has always been so. This teaching is not one for the masses. It has always been available. Ramesh didn't make this up. He is not saying anything new. The underlying tenets of all the major religions are the same. "Hear O' Israel, the Lord our God, the Lord is One." "The Father and I are One." "Tat Twam Asi." "All Roads Lead to Allah." All of the pointers are there. It is not a matter of not *wanting* to see. It is not being *able* to. It is there! People come into Ramesh's talks. I've watched thousands of them come into his talks, sit there, listen to what he has to say, nod their head and go away. No impact. The Resonance is not there. That connection is not there.

So we don't really make our decisions?

The understanding is that every decision is a programmed response, that these decisions that get made are simply the programmed responses of a body-mind mechanism that has certain genetic characteristics at conception, and then has the subsequent experiences which are called, 'conditioning.' So, you have these dual factors of heredity and conditioning which combine to form this organism in this moment. This organism, in this moment, will decide things based on a whole host of conditions and characteristics over which it had no control in putting there in the first place. Therefore you will 'choose' one way in one moment and entirely differently in the very next moment.

I'm sure you've seen an example of this on the highway. You're driving along and somebody cuts you off. You were just thinking about the great time you had the night before—you're in a good mood and everything's going your way. And this guy snakes into the flow of traffic in your lane and you hit the brake and you drive on. No immediate reaction, really. But then the guy turns around at the stoplight and flips you his middle finger! He sticks his head out and says: "You asshole, you didn't let me in! What the fuck's the matter with you?!" Now your adrenaline's all up, right? You're in the fight or flight mode. You were unjustly accused and you've got all this adrenaline in your body. Then a few blocks down the road somebody else cuts you off. What's your reaction now? Your reaction is very likely to be a very intensely antagonistic one. You're pissed off at *this* guy, and so you flip *him* the finger and honk your horn! The same event separated by moments, and yet, your reaction is entirely different because the organism has changed. The organism that is reacting, in the moment when all the adrenaline is running, has changed. So, what I'm saying is that the mechanism reacts or 'chooses' in the moment, according to its nature in the moment, and that that nature changes instant to instant.

I agree one hundred percent that I have no control over the specific result of anything. It seems, though, that we have control over a sort of general intention of the direction of our lives. What I'm saying is that although I agree that I can't control any specific outcome, I feel that

I have some choice over just the general sort of direction that I'm walking. And then whatever the hell happens, happens.

But when you fade things out to that amorphous of a composition whereby you say, "Well, my general intention is to move this way..." there's really no talking about it because there's no action that you can point to which is involved in the process. If there's a specific action that you can point to which is involved, then you can ask yourself if that is truly your unconditioned action. But if it's just an amorphous generalized thing, then there's really nothing to talk about. So, if you can tell me what it is that you are talking about when you say 'a generalized movement in a particular direction—what *constitutes* that generalized movement—then maybe we can look at it and see whether it's a reasonable proposition.

I guess I would define 'generalized movement' by deciding to sit in meditation in the morning and nurturing my highest inner voice.

Well, it is clear that that body-mind mechanism does certain things. It meditates...most mornings?

Yes.

When you meditate in the morning, what is the general result of that?

I'm calmer.

So, your life gets better in general?

Yeah, in general.

And when you don't meditate in the morning, what tends to happen?

I find that if I don't stay connected to some kind of spiritual practice, I just drift away and I'm just not on my own team.

So, why would you choose to *not* meditate in the morning if meditating in the morning makes your life so much better?

(laughs) That's a very complicated question. I ask David that every time I come to lie on his table.

And what does he tell you?

I remember him saying something about why we don't do certain things, but are rather always drawn to a weakened state as if by the Devil...

The Devil? Maybe you're inhabited by the Devil! Ah-ha ! *(laughter)* But if, in fact, you have this choice to shift your attention towards the good, why don't you *do* it ?

(laughing) I think it's the fifty-one percent factor— that if you do fifty-one percent, then you're in good shape. I mean, it's resistance. Why does the alcoholic continue to drink?

I *know* why the alcoholic continues to drink. I was an alcoholic for nineteen years.

And why is that?

Because the body-mind mechanism was alcoholic, and had not been given the Grace to not have to drink. After a few years of drinking alcoholically, your life is screwed up, so you look at it and you say, "My life is screwed up," but you still can't stop drinking—just as *you* say: "When I meditate, my life gets better," yet you still can't meditate every day. So meditation either happens through that body-mind mechanism—at which point certain benefits accrue—or it doesn't, and certain other actions accrue because the body-mind is an instrument through which actions happen. And if there's a sense of personal doership there, if the Divine Hypnosis is there, you say, "*I* decided to meditate today," or "Because of my demons, *I* decided to blow it off today, and *I* will decide to do it better tomorrow."

And you don't believe that at all?

Well, I just haven't found anybody who's able to show me differently.

ᏋᎬ   ᏋᎬ   ᏋᎬ

PAST, PRESENT AND FUTURE ARE NOW

It seems clear that there is no choice but somehow I question the idea of things being predetermined.

Predetermination is a concept. If you don't like that concept, don't use it. Pick another one. There are a million of them.

Okay, but it seems that certain actions come out of conditioning and others come out of an awareness, an openness.

That is right, the conditioning does change.

But doesn't that come from being more open?

This opening is a result of additional conditioning. You see things, you meet a teacher, you read a book, you experience this peace, and thus your conditioning is changed. Those experiences, those thoughts, all of those things change your conditioning. Your conditioning changes every instant.

It seems though, that in that open space habits have more of a chance to drop away.

Perhaps, but the openness is itself a result of conditioning. And I can tell you now from experience that 'habits' such as drinking can fall away without there being any openness, any sense of openness at all.

So you're saying that it is all predetermined?

This whole notion of predetermination is a concept. If we understand that 'It all Is,' then you can see that it is only your experience of it that happens in duration. The model Ramesh uses is of a painting that is fifty miles long...or maybe he says it's five miles, ten miles, whatever...it's a long painting! *(laughter)* In its entirety, it's longer than you can see if you're standing next to it. What is required for you to view this painting is space and time. As you move along the painting, the action which precedes the subsequent action in the painting, is said to have caused it. You say, "Okay this one 'caused' that one, which caused that one, which caused that one." And this is viewed through time. If you step back from the painting far enough, what you see is that it is all there. All the actions have always been there. The whole thing came up at once. Where then is the question of predetermination? Predetermination is only relevant for the one viewing the painting as sequence and even then it is notional. Time is required for its perception.

So the future is already here?

It's all here, past, present and future, it is all here. Now! In this eternal present.

I used to get stuck when someone predicted that this body-mind mechanism was going to die on such and such

date, but you are saying that it is already there, that makes
sense to me.

Did I make sense to you? I never want it to make
sense to you. *(laughter)*

But it seems clear that it is the case.

No! That is just an image that I put forward as a
pointer to bring you possibly to Here!

♋　　♋　　♋

WHAT ABOUT DISCIPLINE?

So what do you think about discipline? Aggressive-
ly disciplining yourself, whether it be physical discipline
or spiritual discipline?

I think that discipline happens through certain
body-mind mechanisms. Certain body-mind mechanisms
are created with tremendous senses of discipline. Now,
there are certainly frequent attempts to take someone
who is slovenly and slothful by nature and *make* them
disciplined. *(laughter)* They are told,"You *should* be disciplined!" But unless their nature has that component of
discipline in it, discipline is not going to happen. And
there may indeed be a component of discipline there that
can be developed. I'm not saying that doesn't happen.
But in utilizing practices that are supposed to develop
discipline, the results vary. If there are two body-mind
mechanisms performing the exact same practice, doing
the same exact thing, one will develop discipline and the
other one won't. And you can come up with all kinds of
reasons, "Well, this one's character is inferior, he's a
screw-up and he didn't try hard enough, he wasn't earnest enough," and all of that. But fundamentally it was

because he didn't have that component there to begin with. It wasn't part of his character, it wasn't part of his nature.

Here's a lamb-chop for the tiger. I understood Ramana—for a while anyway—to say, "You've got no freedom whatsoever, but the only freedom you have got is to find out who you are."

Okay. Who am I to argue with Ramana? *(laughter)* So if you can do that, by all means do! Still, that sounds to me like a pretty big 'but.'

I find that sometimes, asking, "Who am I?" especially when I am totally identified with what's going on, helps me to move up the greasy pendulum shaft.

Sure. That kind of inquiry will very often lead to a 'higher' state of awareness. So, why is it that you DON'T inquire all the time?

That's what I wondered. I suppose it's really not up to me. Sometimes I can't do it, and sometimes it happens by itself.

Yes! Because if you could do it all the time, and it yielded these wonderful results, you'd be *crazy* not to be doing it! So either you are crazy, or you don't have the capacity to determine when you can inquire and when you can't. Even that is given to you.

The only problem is that when I don't inquire, I start worrying about it, that I'm not doing my part in all this.

Sometimes you worry about it, sometimes you don't. The worry sometimes happens. The worry sometimes doesn't happen. And sometimes lunch happens! *(laughter)* And blessedly this is one of those times. Let's go eat!

♋   ♋   ♋

POWERLESSNESS

Last Friday my dad had a physical problem and had to be taken to the hospital. I was sitting there thinking that in the past, I would have been either trying to send him healing energy or asking God for some help. But now my belief is that everything's already done, everything's already happened. And in a way, I feel kind of power-less—which we are, I guess, but it just came as a shock, because that was the first time I'd really had something like that happen where this whole new way of thinking entered into the equation.

Actually, true powerlessness carries with it no frustration whatever. It is the feeling of quasi-powerfulness that causes the frustration. The idea that you have limited power, causes frustration. The conviction that you can truly do nothing, brings with it a sense of enormous peace and contentment if it's purely understood. You rest easily and comfortably in the knowledge that everything is happening precisely the way it's supposed to, and could not be happening any differently. But if there is not pure understanding, then there is a sense that what is happening now is not right, and you need to *do* something about that. And if *you* are not sufficiently powerful by your own unaided effort, then you need to invoke a more powerful source to take care of it." And so you say, "God, do my bidding! Help me out here, this has gotten a little bit beyond me." Now that movement towards acknowledging the power of God is positive to the extent that you are at least acknowledging some kind of limitation to your own power. But in order for there to be peace, you have to then go on to the next step of recognizing that God has *all* of the power. You must realize that even your prayer to God is only God praying to Himself. It is a movement in Consciousness through which something happens, and you are simply the instrument of that activity. So in any given situation, you do what you do. If a prayer comes, a prayer comes, and as to the effect of that prayer—who knows?

Yeah, but it just all of a sudden hit me that this is the way I now think. It was clear that I really grasped this and now was just kind of going with it.

Yes, like you I had always maintained that I was basically the center of the universe with enormous power, and that pretty much anything I set my mind to do, I could do. This was the principle upon which I operated for most of my life. I felt that God was for weaklings, and was a concept that people had created just to make life more bearable for themselves, and that I certainly didn't need anything like that because...I'm *me* ! *(laughter)* which was all well and good until one day my infant son had a very, very high fever, and while we were sitting watching television he went into a convulsion. So, I rushed out of the house with him and drove to the emergency room at the hospital, leaning on the horn and going through all the stop signs and red lights on the way there. I pulled up to the emergency room and handed him through the window of the nurses' station for them to *do* something, and they took him into the back and said, "Have a seat, we'll be with you." And I remember going outside and praying. All my fervent atheism disappeared in that moment. I think it's very natural that when we're face-to-face with our own limitation, our inability to control the world, the most natural thing to do is to attempt to extend our reach by making some kind of deal with God, to invoke God and say, "This time, God, if you get me through *this* one, I promise I'll be better, I'll do whatever You want. Let's make a deal." *(laughter)* The blessing is to be able to sit in fear with the profound awareness of the limitation of this body-mind mechanism as an individual, and to see that, "Yes, everything is unfolding precisely the way it is *supposed* to be unfolding, even when the way it is unfolding is not how I would want it."

Ꮟ   Ꮟ   Ꮟ

IF I HAVE NO CONTROL, WHY BOTHER?

I read some books that say that all the money you're going to have is like your breath—it's written out before-hand. So if there is only going to be a certain amount, why worry about it? Why make any big effort? It's going to come anyway.

But the effort may be part of it coming to you.

Yeah, it's like a double-edged sword. I'm financially at a point right now where I'm just trying not to worry. But I think it's kind of the same for all aspects of life, we shouldn't worry, exert undue effort, or become mentally agitated because whatever is going to happen is going to happen anyway.

Including the worrying, including the mental agitation.

Well...yeah, okay. That's a real tricky, hard one.

It's not tricky at all.

But we don't like to worry.

That's irrelevant. *(laughter)* Your liking it or not liking it is of no consequence whatsoever.

Yet the question always comes, "What is the implication? What's the consequence of this? What do I do now?"

That is a very common question.

From your standpoint, it is all working out as it should. And yet you've still got to carry on with your life, somehow. It seems to me we all want something to do, need to do something.

And you will!

Being told it doesn't matter, my first response is, well I might as well go to sleep, or do nothing, or...um...

Try it! TRY IT! I'm serious, try it. See what happens. Try doing nothing. Try sitting somewhere and doing nothing. See how long you can do it! Your bowels are going to start to insist that you do something. Your body carries certain dictates of hunger, thirst. It will require that you do things to satisfy it.

Okay, well you do certain things like eating and going to the toilet to keep your body going, which are imperative. But with things like the things one reads in books, injustice, requiring social action...anything outside my own personal comfort, so to speak, why would I bother?

Because you live in a society. You've been conditioned in certain ways. This body-mind mechanism carries within it, its own imperatives. So when you read a book about child abuse, you may respond by saying, "I'm going to do something about this. This can't be allowed to continue." Someone else, with a different conditioning, reads the book and says, "This is too depressing," and doesn't get past the first three pages.

Ramesh tells a funny story that relates to this. He usually tells it when the discussion turns to personal responsibility and the nature of doing what is right. He tells the story that Brigitte Bardot was watching television one day in Italy. A program came on about the

clubbing to death of baby harp seals and she was so appalled by this sight that she started a movement that
eventually got this practice stopped. Now it was report-
ed separately that Krishnamurti was watching television
and a similar program featuring the brutal clubbing of
baby harp seals came on. Krishnamurti watched it for a
moment and he was so appalled that he said, "Turn off
the television I can't bear to look at this." So the question
is, how is it that one body-mind mechanism given the
name of Brigitte Bardot reacted to this sight with a particular kind of action and the other body-mind
mechanism of the name Krishnamurti reacted as it reacted? Do you care to hazard a guess on this one?

*I would say it is due to their enculturation. I mean
that would be a very simple answer, but more or less.*

I would agree with you. The programming of the
two organisms was such that when one viewed the scene
it responded with a certain kind of action, and when the
other viewed the same scene it responded with a different action. And the responses were due to the nature of
the organisms in that moment. If viewed on another day
at another time the responses of the two organisms could
be flip-flopped! So the question then is, how do these
natures come about? How do these characters come
about? How does this enculturation come about? Is it
something that we choose to do or is it something that
happens without our input, without our desiring it to
happen, without our necessarily having anything to do
with it? The presumption is if we *did* have the choice in
these matters, we would choose so that our enculturation, and our character would be perfect. If I got to choose
how my responses would be I would certainly tend to
choose the ones that everybody liked, that would make
me a popular guy, that would make people love me, that

would make me feel good about myself and all the rest of it.

Having a couple of children myself, I have had the opportunity to watch how two different organisms given the same basic genetic material can be born with very different temperaments. They were temperamentally different from the outset, from the moment they came out the chute they were different and their personalities became apparent very quickly—far earlier than we could have any chance to impact them by conditioning. So, I am led to believe just from my own experience and a bit of reading on the subject that one's genetics have a tremendous responsibility for how you are, how you react to things. Whether you are an easy going sort or you are an intense sort, whether you hold on for all you're worth or you let go and let it flow. These are programmed into you. Now, various happenings can occur along the way that can change, augment and alter that basic conditioning. Sometimes, it is in a very dramatic way, sometimes in a very subtle way, but the underlying theme is that the response that we say is 'our response' is, in fact, very much a programmed response. It is simply a function of the nature of the organism at that particular instant. It is responding. And what characterizes this response from the standpoint of 'me,' of the individual is that the individual claims doership. The individual claims, "This is my action. That is my response. I did that. I thought that." And this is a very potent experience, a very potent subjective sense that, "I am doing. These are my choices."

In spite of the fact that you can look at how you respond to things and you can look and see how those responses have been conditioned or programmed or dictated by some other events of which you have no control—in spite of that you say, "I chose...I decided."

♋   ♋   ♋

WHAT IF THE DIVINE
HYPNOSIS CEASED EVERYWHERE?

It seems it wouldn't make any difference if your message became clear to everybody, because the mind-body mechanisms would still act in the same way.

Certainly the mind-body mechanisms will behave in the way that they are destined to, which is to say that their behavior will be, in that moment, precisely according to the dictates of that moment.

So, how would it be different if everybody realized that they are not the doer?

There has been quite a lot of speculation on that particular question. Now, Ramesh suggests that if that were the case then the whole manifestation as we know it would collapse, that the play would be over, the curtain would be down and it would be a done deal.

What would that look like?

Who knows? Now my speculation (and it is really just a kind of entertaining mental game) is that the manifestation would go on as long as there was some point of sentience. As long as there was some mechanism with senses, then there would be a phenomenal manifestation. The sense of personal doership is not necessary for there to be a manifestation of this world. This life and living as we know it and think about it in human terms, would not happen, but there could well be a manifestation independent of human beings. There just has to be some point from which the manifestation can be perceived, some mechanism of perception.

This is so different from what a lot of sages would say. They would like for everybody to be enlightened and try to enlighten as many people as they can. The idea being that if everybody is enlightened it would be a very beautiful world. Are you saying that is not the case?

Well, I would hate to be aligned with the, "Let's not enlighten everybody" camp, as small as that camp may be. *(laughter)* I mean, if the proposition and the premise is that if everybody is enlightened that would be the end of suffering, then to work for the enlightenment of all is to work for the elimination of suffering. What could be nobler than that! Personally, I have no agenda. I do not presume to know what is best for the universe.

Are you saying that you wouldn't want to end suffering?

All I am saying is that suffering happens! Suffering is part of What Is. So, if a particular mechanism is programmed in such a way that when it sees suffering it responds to ease that suffering, it will do so! If it is programmed in such a way that it is unaffected by the suffering of others, it won't do anything. So, we have a value system in which those who eliminate the suffering of others are held in high regard and those who cause suffering to others are held in low regard (not always, but generally so). Therefore, if you have a choice, I would say by all means choose to be held in high regard, choose to help others, choose to be a nice person, do all of that. The problem is, I don't think you have a choice. I think if you had a choice, a true choice, everyone would choose that which was in their own best interest which would be to be nice to everybody, to eliminate suffering, to be kind.

So, if I can do that, it's better to do it, right?

If you can, and you think it's better, by all means do.

It makes a lot of sense, just makes sense that, "I am not doing this." I didn't try to get the service award they just gave me, I mean, it just happened. It just happened.

Yes.

I appreciate the part I've been given to play though. (laughter)

Yes.

It is pretty cool. I'm out there helping but I know, I understand and now, sometimes, there is a glimpse, that I'm just being led here. That this is just a play and I'm part of the play and that is why I'm...just OK! I'm not special. So I just enjoy!

When there is that acceptance, then it is pretty peaceful. It is a nice place.

ᥣ   ᥣ   ᥣ

HOW CAN WE
USE THIS TEACHING?

Is there anything that we can do with this teaching?

Not a goddamn thing. All kinds of things *may be done* with this teaching. The effects of the teaching could be revolutionary, but 'you' can't utilize it for your own purposes. Consciousness is utilizing it for Its purposes.

For example, what would happen if I took the thought or concept that, "I can't do anything for myself," and I reminded myself of that over and over again throughout the day, and that notion became very ingrained within me and I worked with it constantly?

It would have an effect.

It would *have some effect.*

I'm not discounting that for an instant. Your ability to *do* that is what I'm questioning.

I'm questioning that, too.

Good!

I doubt if I could do that in the first place.

'You' couldn't *do* it, but it could *happen*. If it happened, then chances are that you would respond very differently in situations than you do now, but that hasn't happened. If it happens, then you will respond differently. Until that time, you will respond according to the way that you are currently conditioned to respond.

Someone told me that Ramesh once said that even though you're not the doer, to act as if you are.

He said that after he was *bludgeoned! (laughter)* The seeker is saying, "I know what you're saying is true, yet I still have this sense of personal doership. I'm stuck with it! So, what do I do?" He said, "You act as if you're the doer." Which is an easy thing to say—you're going to act as if you're the doer anyway! *(laughter)*

And actually his most important bit of advice, he borrowed from the poet, e.e.cummings, who said, "If you can just be, *be*! If not, cheer up and go about other people's business, doing and undoing unto them until you drop!"

☙   ☙   ☙

The truth will set you free. But before it does, it will make you angry.

Jerry Joiner

♋   ♋   ♋

Dear ones,
You who are trying to learn
The Miracle of Love
Through the use of reason,
I am terribly afraid
You will never see the point.

Hafiz

♋   ♋   ♋

Ram Tzu knows this:
Directions are only needed
By those with a destination.

♋   ♋   ♋

The gulf between knowledge and truth is infinite.

Henry Miller

♋   ♋   ♋

Oh bless the continuous stutter of the Word being made into flesh.

Leonard Cohen

As you walk the
Spiritual path
It widens
Not narrows
Until one day
It broadens
To a point
Where
There is no
Path left at all.
Wayne.

♋ ♋ ♋

You delight in being told
You're on the right track
But Ram Tzu knows this
Your train isn't going anywhere.

♋ ♋ ♋

As I walked my spiritual path
I passed many signposts
Left by seekers who had
Passed this way before me.
All pointed onward toward the Truth.

Camped at the base of each
Was a mass of people
Who had stopped
And were now worshipping
The sign.

Wayne

♋ ♋ ♋

Suppose someone were to say, "Imagine this butterfly exactly as it is, but ugly instead of beautiful."

Ludwig Wittgenstein

FIVE

PATHS

ACCEPTANCE

What do you mean when you talk about 'acceptance'?

When acceptance comes, it cuts off involvement, and then there's peace. It isn't the momentary peace you get from getting what you want. And it isn't the peace that is oblivion. Rather it is the peace at the center of the storm, the eye of the hurricane. All around is the swirl of life and living, and the tumult that life is, but in the eye of the storm there's peace. There's quiet. This acceptance I am pointing to is synonymous with that peace and that quiet.

So, having identified that, all we have to do is accept! *(laughter)* It's so simple. Nothing to it, right? Perhaps you've noticed that acceptance is unpredictable. You can't do it yourself! Despite your very best intentions, your most earnest efforts, acceptance has a way of slipping out of your grasp. Acceptance *comes,* as does nonacceptance. It comes. The acceptance *can* come at any instant without warning, without preparation.

But you cannot manufacture it. And the recognition that you can't manufacture it, is itself acceptance. Acceptance can arise at any moment, and cut off the horizontal involvement. And the cutting off of that horizontal involvement is peace. Now, if there's any value in the intellectual understanding, it is that it *can* arise in mind and bring about acceptance and the understanding that *All is Consciousness,* that everything that is happening could not be otherwise. This is not to say that it won't change in the next instant. But in *this instant* it could not be otherwise. And the recognition of that is acceptance, the recognition that *this IS,* is peace.

It has nothing to do with approval. I'm not saying that you have to *like* it. The acceptance can be of something that's utterly horrible, tragic, painful. And amidst the horror, the tragedy, the pain, there can be peace. And the peace is in the acceptance, in the recognition that IT IS, in this moment.

When it happens, we say it's Grace. This understanding, this acceptance, this cutting off of involvement, this peace, is Grace. Now Grace, of course, is a very fancy spiritual term for 'good luck'! *(laughter)* When it's going our way, when it provides us with something that's personally satisfying, we say it's Grace. When it's awful, we say it's God's will. *(laughter)* But the great thing about either of those terms is the recognition that,"I didn't do it." I as a separate doer, didn't do it. There was some agency other than my will at work.

When I met Ramesh, and he was talking about this, I found it to be incredibly liberating because most of the teachings that I'd been encountering up until that time seemed to exist in some sort of vacuum that didn't ac-

count for THIS. Somehow, all the spiritual stuff was removed from THIS. THIS, *this* life and this living, this
day-to-day activity, *this* going to work, and making love,
and yelling at the dog, and having a meal, and all of
those things, were somehow profane, when compared
to the exalted spiritual presence. And what Ramesh was
saying, quite clearly, was that THIS was sacred. The manifestation in all of its characteristics, both positive and
negative, the ones we like and the ones we don't; the
ones we approve of and the ones we don't, the ones we
would change and the ones we wouldn't. All of those
things, every aspect of the phenomenal manifestation *is
sacred* and carries with it the imprint of God.

Ramesh was a banker. The man was a banker! He
lived in the world. He was married. He had children.
His spirituality was one that encompassed all of THIS.
And it made sense to me, it resonated with me, it *rang
true* with me. I wasn't interested in a spirituality that
required me to go sit in a cave, have things eat at my
flesh as a testament to how spiritual I was. That seemed
ludicrous. And it *is* ludicrous if that is done deliberately,
to achieve something.

There was a Zen master who was widely quoted
who taught, "You chop wood and carry water." I came
to understand that he was talking about your work. Today, the water and the heat are supplied. The work is to
go hammer on a computer terminal. Your work is to go
teach something to a group of people. Your work is to go
pump gas. Whatever your work is, that's chopping wood
and carrying water, that's doing THIS. That's doing life.

God's here. Right here. In this moment, in this place.
You don't necessarily have to go to India. Thank God!
(loud laughter)

In fact, this morning somebody asked about what
changed after this sense of personal doership fell away.
What was it, what was that about? Frankly, when it hap-

pened, the clearest sense was that literally, nothing had happened, very profoundly, NOTHING HAD HAPPENED. And this much desired enlightenment was not *anything*. It was literally nothing. And six or eight months later I was in India, with Ramesh, and talking to him about this enlightenment business, and I said "You know, if someone were to ask me, 'Are you enlightened?' I guess I would have to say no." And he broke in with, "You would have to say, 'No, *but there is Understanding here.'*" It was just the perfect turn of phrase. No. There are no enlightened individuals. But there is Understanding *here*. Not here, *(pointing to his body)* Here! *(pointing to the space in front of him)*. And that Understanding manifests, is made palpable, in the connection with one who comes seeking, the one who wants to know, and in that inquiry finds Resonance, finds this connection. Then the Guru exists. The Guru is created in that relationship. In its absence, there is simply a body-mind mechanism, like any other, that goes through its day doing what it does, acting according to its nature, reacting according to its nature, according to the dictates of the moment. The Guru exists *only* in the relationship with the disciple. Otherwise, there is no Guru.

♋   ♋   ♋

EXPERIENCING WHAT IS

Based on your experience, what do you recommend as a way of understanding or knowing What Is?

Well, I would say you should drink and use drugs for nineteen years. *(laughter)* That's what I did! So, what time do the pubs close here? Better get started!

What underlies the question is the notion that "I'm the doer." You say, "Okay, I'm the doer, therefore, what should I do to get what I want?" What is wanted is this Understanding, this Awakening, this elimination of the sense of personal doership. "So tell me, what I should do?" Now there are lots of people who will tell you what you should do. I'm not one of them. Because the presumption in telling you to do something is that you have a wheel connected to something—that if you turn it this way, you can get the boat to go that way. What I'm telling you, what is my experience, what my Guru told me, is that *your wheel is not connected to anything.* Any action that is to be taken through this body-mind mechanism, will happen through this body-mind mechanism. The thought will arise, "I should go and do this." And if it is to happen, the thought will be followed with the means for the action to be effected.

So, the desire arises, the desire to do something does arise, and if that desire arises in a particular body-mind mechanism and the Universe cooperates, then the event happens. When I say, "the Universe cooperates," what I'm saying is that you only apparently decide, "I need a teacher." The thought comes, "I need a teacher. There is a teacher coming. I'm going to go see him." The thought arises, the desire arises, the impulse arises. The decision is made through this body-mind mechanism to go see that teacher. Now, whether that decision results in your actually seeing the teacher depends on a staggering number of other things happening which are totally outside your control.

♋   ♋   ♋

ALCOHOL AND DRUGS AS *SADHANA*?

It seems to me that drinking and drugging would be a great entree to Enlightenment because when you are drugged or drunk you give up the body mind complex. You let go of it. You let go of it again and again and again. Eventually it must become easier to do this in a meditative state.

I'm not all together certain that is the case. I mean the alcohol and drugs might do the job, but it doesn't have to do with the alcoholic or drug addict letting go or even intending to. None of the bars or dope houses I went to were full of *jnanis!*

The notion of letting go of the mind-body mechanism is kind of an interesting one because one does that with the expectation that one is going to get something...freedom. Generally what seekers are looking for is an escape from suffering and that certainly is a potent desire. I would even go so far as to say that what seekers are looking for is a cessation of pain both psychological, emotional and if you have it, physical.

Or at least from having to direct your life.

Yes, because if directing your life was satisfying and enjoyable all the time you wouldn't be looking for a release from that or a freedom from that.

I don't want to be a doer. I would like to have a release from having to be a doer, at least a temporary release.

Yes. Well, somebody was proposing how cool it would be if you could scamper up the pendulum when things got shitty and then scamper back down the pendulum when things were good so you got the full thrust of the swing into the good stuff. Then when things got a little uncomfortable a little unhappy and a little painful, you could scamper up into oblivion and you wouldn't have to experience any of that.

That is why people take a drink when they get a Dear John letter.

Bingo! Or sit down to meditate or do one of a thousand things to make the pain less.

Wouldn't scampering up the pendulum make the better times even better, or is it that because you're not attached to it you wouldn't feel it as much, you wouldn't experience it, you wouldn't take as much possession of it?

Exactly, that is why that principle, that model is suggested because it is the impersonality of the experience at the top of the pendulum which carries with it its own quality, but it is not the rush and the fun of a really good time.

Like winning a million bucks or something.

Yes, but everything which has a bit of an adrenaline rush associated with it, contains its conditioned opposite which is a lousy time.

Seems like a good plan to me, this scamper up routine!

Of course, for the most part, that is really what you try and do throughout your life with your day to day activities…maximize what you like, minimize what you don't.

♋   ♋   ♋

HOW ENLIGHTENMENT LOOKS

Bhagwan Shree Rajneesh said that he himself was enlightened, and that he could smoke cigars and drink beer and do all kinds of things and still be enlightened, that it wasn't going to affect his Enlightenment one bit.

Really! (laughter)

Really. And people bought that too.

I buy it too. I don't think there is any particular code of behavior that determines Enlightenment.

He sounds an awful lot like Ikkyu.

(another questioner) Like who?

Ikkyu. He was a Zen monk of the fourteenth to fifteenth century who one day just finally had it, and told the people at his monastery: "I've had it with you guys. If you want me, I'm going to be down at the whorehouse." And he spent the rest of his days down there, writing poetry and enjoying life.

That sounds a little addictive. Is it possible to be addicted and at the same time enlightened?

See, you're thinking in terms of an enlightened individual, but there are no enlightened individuals. There are no enlightened body-mind mechanisms. There is no enlightened meat. But it always comes back to this: "What is it going to be like for *me* when *I'm* enlightened? If I can find someone who's enlightened and I ask them what it's like for them, then I can get some idea of what it's like and whether it's going to be worth it, whether I should even bother." (laughter) And then of course the following question is, "How did *you* get there? I'll follow your path." Well, I was an alcoholic and a drug addict for nineteen years. That was my 'path.'

When a small group of us were talking to Ramesh about the different *yogas* and different *sadhanas*, I told him the story of what my life had been like. How one night I had been struck sober in the middle of the night after many years of full-on alcoholism and drug addiction, and how that started me on the spiritual path. I had to find out what had done that to me. What was it that had just utterly and completely transformed me when I always thought that I was the one who was doing all the actions, that everything was my choice—that I was the chooser, the doer? When I was 'struck sober' it was clear that *I* hadn't done it. It had *happened* to me, so, I set about finding out what did that, and within a year and a half that led me to Ramesh. So I got there with very little spiritual background, and I said, "All these people around here have been at this for ten, fifteen, twenty years. They've been to Rajneesh, they've been to Muktananda, they've been zapped with peacock feathers, they've walked around Arunachala, they've had spiritual sex until they were too sore to walk, they can even spell 'Nisargadatta'—*they* can do *all* this trick stuff, and *I* hardly know *anything!*" *(laughter)* So, then Ramesh told me about *sadhana*, and he explained that the *sadhana* of this particular body-mind mechanism had been to drink and use drugs for nineteen years until its ego structure was beaten to the point where it could accept the notion that perhaps there was something more. That was *my sadhana*. And if someone asks, "How did it happen for you?" well, that's what happened in the twenty years prior. Do what *I* did for twenty years! Though, lots of people were sitting next to me on bar stools during those years. Many of them are dead now. One man's *sadhana* is another man's death march. So, go figure! *(laughter)*

♋   ♋   ♋

SEEKING A TECHNIQUE

I find it very hard to let go of the body-mind mechanism.

Who told you to do that? Is it your premise that the goal of spirituality is to let go of the mind-body mechanism? To stop being the doer?

Isn't that the goal? To stop being the doer?

You were never the doer. How can you stop being the doer?

I thought I was the doer. It is hard to stop thinking as the doer.

Yes, but again any time that you are letting go of something, this implies doership. Whether you find it difficult to let go of it, or you find it easy to let go of it, there is a 'you' doing that.

So, it is irrelevant.

Essentially.

That is beautiful thank you.

♋

My desire is to give that sense of personal doership up. I'd love to believe the Ramesh model and your model, I'd really like to believe that.

YOU would like to give it up?

Yeah!

Hear what you're saying!

But it's not happening. In me, it's conditional.

Yes. And it only can *happen*...

There has to be acceptance...?

Acceptance. Well, this is what we are talking about. Acceptance that this is, in fact, the case, that it can only happen. That Acceptance, *when* it happens, is incredibly freeing. It is deep and it is profound when it happens. You cannot manufacture it. If you could, you *would!* Everybody would.

So, one sits back and waits, it might happen, it might not happen?

No. One does what one does.

One thinks about it?

Maybe. If it's a thinking type of organism it thinks about it. If it is a patient kind of organism it sits back and waits. If it's a devotional kind of organism it sings *bhajans* and offers prayers. If it's a real strong doing kind of organism it goes out and does all kinds of charity work or starts an ashram, or does something else. It depends on the nature of the mechanism. It cannot do nothing, unless it is one of a very few organisms which are programmed in such a way that they actually can sit and do nothing—call 'em yogis, call 'em bums—there are a few who can literally sit and do nothing, but they're rare. Very, very, *very* rare. Most of these other organisms, certainly the ones that are walking around cities like this, and that are dressed like *this*, have to do stuff! *(laughter)*. They are compelled by their natures and circumstances to do things.

♋   ♋   ♋

CONTROLLING EMOTION

Yesterday I became consumed by intense anger over some rabbits that were being neglected and abused. I took action by calling the authorities, but the feeling of intense emotion is still there.

So there *is* intense emotion *there.*

So what do I do with it?

What *needs* to be done with it?

It hurts. I'm uncomfortable with it.

Okay, so there *is* discomfort there.

Right. So does it dissolve on its own if you stay with it?

Isn't it your experience that your discomfort eventually passes? I'm sure this is not the first time that you've ever felt uncomfortable. Chances are that you can't even remember the cause of your discomfort three discomforts ago.

Yes, it dissolves, but that doesn't answer anything. All right, I guess what I'm saying is that I don't want to be so reactive. That's what it is. I want to get out of it and stop all this intense reaction to the pain and suffering in the world. I don't want to suffer that way. So I read more Ramesh, and I come here, yet I still react!

Yes. So you have either not been able to locate a good enough technique despite many years of diligent effort, or you are stuck with who you are until such time as your conditioning, your programming changes.

Yes, you told me before that I'm stuck with it, but I don't like being stuck with it. It hurts.

But pain comes with the territory. There is no way out of pain. As long as there is Consciousness flowing through that body-mind mechanism, there will be pain. There will be pleasure and there will be pain.

Yes, I guess I just have to surrender to it and accept it, although I am stuck and hurting terribly.

At this instant you do not appear to be 'hurting terribly.'

At this instant? No, I'm not. I meant when I was experiencing that. But as you said, pain is part of life.

Yes, although if the thought arises that, 'pain is part of life,' then that will help to mitigate the pain, or more precisely cut off the suffering that comes from involvement with the pain. And you can see from this very experience that the pain comes *and* it goes.

Yes. Well...(reflecting) Wow! I need to try that out again!

Okay. Report back! *(laughter)*

Now I feel very good.

This too shall pass.

♋   ♋   ♋

ADVAITA VEDANTA

You're teaching the path of Advaita Vedanta, aren't you...Ramana Maharshi, and that lineage?

More or less. A fellow interviewed me a couple of weeks ago and he asked precisely that question about this notion of lineage. And because of my own western orientation, and the fact that I was not schooled in Hinduism or in the Eastern tradition, my teaching reflects that. I only studied Eastern spirituality for a year or so before I met Ramesh. Prior to that I'd been a drunk and a drug addict for nineteen years. That was basically what *I* was up to. *(laughs)* Spirituality, hanging around in ashrams, and listening to stuff like this was not of much interest to me. Since I don't come from a rich, long, deep immersion into that structure and into that subculture, the connection to it is minimal.

Now, the teaching that happens through this body-mind mechanism, is very much an expression of one who has been an alcoholic and a drug addict, and a business man, and who has lived in the world, and had a family, and then became interested in spirituality and then had this Awakening happen through it. Therefore, the way that this Understanding is articulated through this body-mind mechanism has only the most tenuous connection to all of the Indian spiritual history. You see? This Understanding happened through, you could say, the Grace of my Guru, Ramesh. In my connection with him, there was this first glimmering of acceptance. I got a sense of what was beyond this manifestation, underlying it, what it is an expression of.

And the context that I put it in, was reflective of who I was. It was not the context of Ramana Maharshi, who was an Indian Hindu living in Southern India. Nor Nisargadatta Maharaj, who was a Hindu living in Bombay. Or even Ramesh, who is a Hindu Brahman, living in India. Now, the fact that Ramesh was educated in London, and was the president of a bank, (a huge bank, the Bank of India, which, at that time, had five thousand employees) who was married and had children, and lived a 'whole' life, made him more accessible. There was an experiential bridge there that I could cross over with him, that would never have been there for me with Maharaj or Ramana Maharshi.

What you'll find is that where there is the absence of Intuitive Understanding, all that is left is the parroting of the teaching of the previous Guru. As a teacher, all you can do is repeat what he said, and you say, "Well, I believed him. My experience with him is that he spoke the Truth. This is what he said. This must be the Truth. Here it is. And he *(clapping)* sang these songs, and he dressed this way and looked at people this way. And so I will *(clapping)* sing these songs, and I will dress this way, and look at people this way, and will repeat what he said, and we'll call it 'Advaita,' or we'll call it a 'Search for Truth,' or we will call it 'Satsang,' or whatever, and we'll be searchers after Truth, together, and I will lead."

Lead?

I'll lead, because I've got a stronger personality and a better ability to mimic. *(laughs)* The fact is, until you are living the truth, until it's yours, you can only mouth the words of other people, or if you are fortunate enough to be carrying forward a silent tradition, keep your mouth shut.

♋   ♋   ♋

THREE NOTIONAL PATHS

Would you talk about the path of jnana?

The path of knowledge or *jnana,* which is nominally what Advaita is about, is often thought to be polarically separated from the path of devotion, but this is not the case. They are clearly extensions of the same Energy, and they just manifest differently according to the basic temperament of the 'individual.' Some people tend to be quite intellectual, and their primary tool for understanding is that of the mind. Thus the path of knowledge is particularly well suited to people with that characteristic. Others tend to be more emotional by nature and they feel things emotionally rather than process them intellectually. For them the path of devotion—the joy found in chanting and being in the presence of the Guru, of surrendering oneself in that way—is more natural and satisfying. But these distinctions are notional. No one is exclusively intellectual by nature, and no one is exclusively emotional by nature. There is a third path as well, which is the path of doing good works, of helping others, of surrendering oneself in the performance of selfless actions. These are the three notional paths (yogas) mentioned in the *Bhagavad-Gita* and other ancient literatures of the Hindu tradition. Personally, I'm not much of a Hindu. In fact, I'm not a Hindu at all! *(laughter)* But inevitably because my teacher comes from that tradition, and I've edited his books and been immersed in his teaching, (which *is* grounded in the Hindu tradition) I've gotten some of it. But I have not taken a Hindu name or begun wearing special clothes because that just doesn't feel right for me. *(laughter)* I don't have anything against it. It's just not my deal.

At any rate, those three paths—*jnana-yoga*, *bhakti-yoga*, and *karma-yoga*—are the notional distinctions that are made in describing the 'ways' of the seeker. And frequently, a seeker will move from an emphasis on one path to another, and I am told that in the Upanishads, it is said that the final movement is onto the path of knowledge. At some point the question arises, "Who is it that is surrendering himself? Who is it that is devoting himself to the Guru? Who is it that is engaging in selfless acts? What is going on here? Exactly *who* is *doing* this?" And that's the question that Advaita picks up. Of course it does a rather poor job of answering the question because ultimately there *is* no answer to it!

ᨀ   ᨀ   ᨀ

SPIRITUAL PRACTICES

MEDITATION

Wayne, could you explain something to me? I've been meditating for a long, long time and when I first started, they talked about transcendence. When you meditate, you go deep into that place which is very comfortable, and they say that that is your way to Enlightenment. If you can go down there, stay there, and bring that out into activity, then you'll release all of your stress. Those are the mechanics of how that works. So, I guess I'm asking your opinion on that space between the thoughts, or transcendence, or whatever you want to call it. Is there anything in the Advaita teachings that mentions this place?

Well, in the model that I use, meditation can sometimes lead to a movement 'up the pendulum shaft.' And so in the state of equanimity where you go inside of yourself, there is peace, and that peace is the absence or reduction, of the sense of personal doership, in that moment. There is just presence—which you can say is the absence of the *doer*, the 'me,' or the diminution of it— and it has very profound benefits to the individual. It feels good.

That's the main thing.

Yes. It makes life more pleasant. As far as I'm concerned, anything that makes life more pleasant is great. But what that all has to do with Enlightenment is another matter entirely.

I don't completely buy into that idea of meditation leading to Enlightenment anymore. I just feel that when I do it, I feel very comfortable. It feels wonderful, and that's basically it.

So what more do you *want?*

Well, I've been studying it again recently, and when-ever I hear someone saying that the way to Enlightenment is by meditating, I feel some uncertainty.

Well, let me ask you, how many people have been meditating worldwide over the last, say, thirty years?

It's been twenty-five years for me.

Twenty-five years, in your own experience. So out of the thousands and thousands and thousands and thousands and thousands of meditators—*very* earnest, *diligent* meditators who have never missed a session—where is all this Enlightenment that this earnest diligent meditation is producing?

It doesn't seem to be happening.

No. *(laughter)* Perhaps they aren't doing it right!

When I meditate, it makes me feel good, so that's it. It's just a comfortable place to go. Someone else sits down and drinks a glass of wine and that's comfortable for them, whereas I sit down and meditate and that's comfortable for me.

Right. And it tends to have fewer side effects too. *(laughter)*

And for me it has more benefits.

Yes, and since that body-mind mechanism receives those benefits from that activity, it tends to continue that activity.

I don't know if I've been doing it so long that it's like an addiction, but when I stopped I didn't feel good, so I just said, "Well, forget this, I'll just continue on meditating," and that's it.

Is there a 'down' side to it? Are there any negatives associated with it?

Well...no.

Then why stop?

It's as simple as that?

It really is as simple as that.

♋

PRAYER

Wayne, what are your thoughts on prayer? If Consciousness is all One, and I pray, is that like talking to myself?

My observation is that prayer *happens*. It happens through body-mind mechanisms as part of this functioning of Totality.

Does prayer work?

Well, you can say that prayer works when it is supposed to work. In other words, if you take it from the other side, you could say, "In order for there to be a healing a prayer is needed." So for this healing to happen a prayer is needed, and the thought arises in this body-mind mechanism to pray. Prayer is offered up, the healing happens. If there's a sense of personal doership in this body-mind mechanism, it will say, "I decided to pray, and my prayer caused the healing." Which is as reasonable a way to look at things as is any, I suppose. And it's certainly a very common and usual way of looking at things. The underlying understanding is that the entire script has been written, including the prayer, including the efficacy of that particular prayer, and the result of that prayer. It is *all* part of this one functioning.

It is only from the standpoint of the individual who considers himself the doer that the question, "Should I pray, or should I meditate?" arises. The underlying presumption being that it is up to me to decide whether to do this or not. What Ramesh would probably tell you is, "If you feel like praying, pray. If you feel like meditating, meditate. If you don't feel like meditating, don't meditate. If you don't feel like praying, don't pray." It is a real safe statement to make. *(laughter)* Because he knows that it's either going to happen or it's not.

♋

SELF INQUIRY

Ramana Maharshi asked the question, "Who am I?" At first I used to struggle with that bit, and then I tried it and it seemed to work. But it seems to me it's another device and yesterday in your talk I realized that the problem really is that I want life to be other than it is. That seems to be the only problem. Once I saw that and accepted it for what it was, it actually became other than it was. It changed.

Yes. Exactly!

So, then what's with the "Who am I?" bit ...?

It was an incredibly potent teaching tool in the hands of Ramana Maharshi. But you're right. It is a conceptual tool. There is nothing inherently *sacred*—I know this is sacrilege—there is nothing inherently sacred about it!

My life has been about learning techniques and doing them well. And I'm concerned about creating a technique out of turning my attention inward. I don't want to create a technique out of it. So, is there some way you can help me to not do that?

No. The turning in happens. Whether it is connected with an objective or not, is also part of What Is, you see. I will not give you a technique to help you stop creating techniques.

♋

SERVING THE GURU

What's the value of serving the Guru in a very personal way if that's possible?

You mean, what will you get out of it?

Well, that might be the question. (laughter)

That's what value means.

Yes, but I get the sense that there is a connection and there is no connection...both. And yet people speak of serving on a personal level, as being a real secret to Awakening, or to knowing Truth. And I wondered what you think of that?

You see, I'm not interested in a mechanistic explanation like, "When you do this, you get that. If you meditate for fourteen years, if you serve the Guru as diligently as you possibly can, if you purify yourself, if you do this, that or the other thing, stand on your head, whatever ."

It's still the same concept.

It's still the notion that if I do this, I will get that. And what I am saying is you do what you do and you get what you get. They aren't necessarily related. If there is Resonance between the body-mind mechanism of the disciple and the body-mind mechanism of the Guru, the disciple can not help but do what he or she does. When

I met Ramesh and I had this unbelievable, unmistakable connection with him, I found myself, for the first time perhaps in my life, actively asking, "What can I do for him?" without any thought of, "What will it get me?" This was not a characteristic thought! *(laughter)* This didn't come to me naturally. I am not generous by nature. It was a surprise! *(laughter)* And yet it was there. It was the purest feeling of love that I've ever had. There was just this desire to give. And it was its own reward, you see.

But isn't it possible through one's conditioning to block the possibility of that connection with the Guru, out of fear or old patterns?

Well, yes. If there's fear, if there are old patterns, if there are blockages then the connection doesn't arise. The selfless desire to give doesn't arise. A desire to give to get arises. You see that all the time. It's just what happens. And ultimately, if you're giving to get, you're probably not going to get what you want, and then you'll have to go elsewhere. Because eventually you'll be disappointed. Even if you get it. *(laughter)*

♋   ♋   ♋

WHEN DESCRIPTION BECOMES PRESCRIPTION

Is it true that you have no methods?

I don't have any methods.

Well, it's like in Zen when they say the method of no-method.

All right. But the instant that you turn no-method into a method, it is no longer no-method. It is a method. And that is, of course, what has been done with various non-methodologies with Zen, Advaita, and Taoism...

With all of them.

They were all, at their root, non-methodological ways of describing What Is. They were subsequently mis-interpreted as prescriptive utterances by various disciples and teachers, who did not have the understanding of the original sage. Oh well...

In Zen there's a saying that "If you meet the Bud-dha, you should kill him."

Absolutely. The Buddha you can meet is not the True Buddha. That correlates to what Lao Tzu said in the first line of the Tao Te Ching, "The Tao that can be named is not the true Tao." Ramana Maharshi describes this process as utilizing a thorn to remove another thorn. So, you use these concepts as you would use a thorn, to remove another thorn that's embedded, let's say, in your foot. And then you throw both thorns away.

Now, the model I use is a scalpel, for a surgeon. You watch a brain surgeon. You sit in the operating the-atre, you look down and he's got his scalpel. He makes an incision in the patient's head, he cuts through the bone, gets down to the brain, he makes the *slightest* inci-sion, just in the right spot, he cauterizes the wound, sews the patient back up again, the patient is carted off, and there is an incredibly dramatic recovery. This patient has the most impressive result. And you sit up there and you watch this happen over and over again. And it's amaz-ing what this scalpel can do! So, one day when the operation is over, you go down, and take the scalpel. Now, you're walking down the street and you meet somebody that has the same symptoms that the surgical patients had, and you say, "I can help you out. I have the scalpel! Just lie down." *(Loud laughter)* You've *watched* what the surgeon does, and you make the incision, you make the incision there and you cut right about there, and you make a bloody mess! Because it ain't the scalpel! And any of you who have been hanging around spiritual circles for any time at all have seen this principle in action. You have watched people imitate the guru saying, "So who wants to know? Who's asking the question?" *(loud long laughter)* As if this Self-inquiry is some kind of magic scalpel that can be applied willy-nilly to obtain these incredible results, and that if you just sit for twenty-four or forty-eight or seventy-two hours in front of somebody else, looking deeply into their eyes saying, "Who am I? Who's asking the question?" then enlightenment will happen! There are actually workshops promising enlightenment over the weekend if you pay to do this!

That is this principle carried to its ultimate ridiculousness. Something will happen. Results of various kinds will happen, but what the hell it has to do with Awakening or Ultimate Understanding is beyond me. This Self-inquiry, this question, "Who is inquiring? Who wants to know?" in the hands of a sage, *can be* incredibly effective, can bring about wondrous transformations, as people saw all the time when Ramana Maharshi utilized it. Of course, the temptation is to think that it is the Inquiry, that it is simply asking the question that does the deed! But it is not so. This is not a technique that can be applied indiscriminately.

I kind of like the humor in the Zen formulation of that because it doesn't really allow you to take the tool too seriously in the search.

Sure, that is why they're yucking it up so much in the Zen monasteries. *(laughter)* But the true Masters always had a lightness about it. The Master always knew that this is all a kind of joke, and that they're just out there doing what they're doing as part of the system. None of the Masters has ever really taken it that seriously. It's only the ones who come after who take the words of the Master and enshrine them. And what happens in the Zen monastery is...well, do you know the story of the *zendo* cat?

No.

A Zen monastery had a mouse problem, so they got a young cat, and the cat did a fine job of getting rid of the mice. But every time the monks would start their sitting practice, the cat would come in and jump from lap to lap and generally make a nuisance of itself. So, what they did was assign a task to the newest acolyte. Before each of the sittings, he was to take the cat and tie it to a post. Then they could sit in peace. This went on for years and years. Monks came and went, a new abbot came, and finally the cat died at the ripe old age of sixteen years. And when the cat died the monastery was thrown into chaos. They couldn't start the meditation. They had to find a cat to tie to the post before they could start their Zen sitting!

Did you ever feel as if, because of the different events that were happening in your life (suddenly you become sober, begin reading spiritual books, then you go and meet Ramesh, then you become the book editor) there was a preparation to the Understanding? I mean as you look back?

Always, in looking back, you can see the connection between things. You can trace the path backwards. You look back, there's the path! But all you can really say about it is that that was *your* path. You can say each step along that path led to the next place on the path.

You can characterize it and say that each step was a preparation for the next place on the path, if you want to put it in those terms. But all it is is a sequence of events. And what you're really looking at is a sequence of events that you're identifying. There are all kinds of other events that escape your attention. Those are just the ones that you would select to write down as part of your biography, if you will. A few significant events that you point to as being the ones that are part of *your* history, part of your path. What we're talking about is history. And history is just the plucking of a couple of events to create a story. But there have been literally *billions* of events in your past that have directly affected you, most of which you aren't even aware of.

So, there is no cause to Enlightenment. Is that correct?

Cause is notional. Cause is arbitrary. Pick an event, any event and with sufficient imagination you can link it to a subsequent event and say that it was the cause. So, you can say there is no cause. Or you can say there were billions of causes.

Is there no recipe in this teaching that would lead to Enlightenment, if it were followed? You use the pointer that Enlightenment is the understanding that there is no separate doer.

That is a *description*. It is not a *prescription*.

If you don't get that concept can you still get enlightened?

Of course. In fact, that concept has to drop in order for the Enlightenment to happen. The Enlightenment can not happen in the presence of that concept.

Yes. But isn't that concept preliminary, even though at the last stage it may obstruct Enlightenment?

Oh you can say it's preliminary if the concept happens to come into your life and subsequently there is Understanding. You can say it was preliminary—it came before. I was a drunk and a drug addict for nineteen years. Would you say that that *caused* the Understanding? If it did, what about all those guys I was drinking with, who are still shit-faced some place, or dead? How do you account for them? So it must not be that. Yet, that was preliminary. That came before.

If I insist that I am the doer, obviously Enlightenment is not going to happen, and my head is not in the tiger's mouth. Is that right?

No, your head *is* in the tiger's mouth. You can insist that you're the doer, or insist that you're not the doer. It is Consciousness that is insisting through you that you're the doer, or insisting through you that you're not the doer. If Understanding is to happen through that body-mind mechanism, it doesn't *matter* what concepts are floating around. They *all* get dissolved in the Understanding (the good ones and the bad ones, the useful ones and the ones that are obstructive). They *all* go.

I have a question about seeking. Ramesh said that if the disciple feels that he has to be near or in the physical presence of the Guru, it's bondage. So, it seems like that seeking, especially passionate seeking, is almost a blockage to Enlightenment, because such seeking implies and reinforces that there is a seeker, and would separate the seeker from What Is.

What Ramesh is saying is that the seeking is not Understanding. This is just another way of saying that as long as there's a seeking, there isn't Understanding.

There is no ultimate Understanding in the presence of the seeking. In the presence of the seeker seeking connection with the Guru, with the One (seeking that *experience* of connectedness, which is a movement up the pendulum shaft) as long as there is that, there cannot be Understanding. He is not saying that *you must rid yourself* of that or that you must *not* go to a Guru, that if it arises you must squash the desire to be with the Guru. He's not saying *any* of that. None of that is implied in his statement of how things *are*. He is simply describing the state of affairs.

So for the 'me' who is caught in the illusion, is there anything to do?

You're caught in the illusion much of the time, right? Would you say so?

Yes.

Is there action? Does action happen through that body-mind mechanism?

Definitely.

Definitely. So, is there anything to *do*? Yes, there are all kinds of things. And what the next action is going to be, you just have to show up and see!

There's that first step, that little bit of awareness, and then I'm caught again. So I guess the general flavor of my question regarding spiritual practices is, ideas, insight, anything that helps you have that awareness that you're going up and down; that's just done? Does the universe do it to you and you have no choice? I mean, I know that's the overall fabric and framework, but it would seem that Consciousness Itself at some point would decide to wake up or not.

Yes, It does. It puts the seeking in a particular body-mind mechanism, and ends the seeking in either that one or another one.

And you don't have any choice about it because 'you' never existed?

And if you had any choice about it, presumably you would have chosen by *now* ! I'm sure it hasn't been for lack of trying.

So, Consciousness 'lives' you until you're done?

Until *It's* done. And That is what you truly *are*. That is all there is. Consciousness is all there is.

I think we should enjoy the waiting process, and not be so concerned about the searching.

It's not a question of 'should.' If you *can*, then that would be a much more comfortable state of affairs than to feel this strong pull to seek. But when the strong feeling arises, there is an irrepressible desire to know.

I think I experienced that about thirty years ago. And I probably spent the better part of ten years trying to fill that need. And I finally exhausted all the avenues. So I quit searching, and at that point I realized that there wasn't anything to look for. I think I got so caught up in the process of trying that I forgot about being.

Mmhm.

And now I'm just being. And I feel that if someone were to ask me, "What's it all about?" I think I would probably have to say, "It's about being right here, right now." And I think that's where the reward is. It's right here, right now. And we have to get in touch with that. And I think there are a lot of distractions.

Mmhm.

And those are the things we have to...I'm not sure what...ignore, or, you know...don't give energy to it. Just swat it away like a fly. Because it's nothing more than a distraction. I'm not trying to teach, I'm just comparing notes.

Ah-ha...well, you know, I'm with you...that...

...This is It.

Sure! *(laughter)* No doubt about that.

I'm having a great time.

Cool! *(laughter)* The thing is that the swatting away of the distractions can only come. The thought either arises to swat the distraction away or you get involved in the distraction. And unless the thought arises, "Oh! This is a distraction! I'll just swat it away," then you're involved in the distraction, and it's a distraction. So, it's clear that if you have the choice, by all means swat it away. But these are intelligent people. They've heard this before, these are not new seekers. They've been at it for a while. They've heard the words: "Be here now. Now is what's happening. This is where it's at." And still the distractions come. The distractions distract.

Maybe that's the reason for the disciplines that the yogis practice, in order to gain control of the moment. Like focus on the concentration, and those things.

Sure.

Maybe there should be some technique that people might try to help them.

There are hundreds of them!

Then they should do them.

Most of these people have done lots of them.

There must be one technique for each individual. Each individual probably has their own way of dealing with the distractions. And I'm afraid most people entertain the distractions.

Why would they do that?

Maybe they find entertainment in the illusion, and so they continue to embrace it. But eventually, like all things, it'll pass.

I agree...this too shall pass.

And then they're stuck with where they were to begin with. So, why not just enjoy where they are, and not chase after the illusions?

Exactly! Why don't they?

I think that's pretty obvious.

It's brutally obvious to everyone here. Most people here would probably want to eliminate suffering, and be at peace. They would like to be present. And yet, despite their most earnest efforts (and you can poll the people afterwards as to the number of techniques that they've employed, and I'm sure you'll get quite a list) the question then becomes, how is it that there is still distraction?

I noticed that you were able to stare into her eyes for three minutes, maybe five.

Mmhm.

We're all here. And we didn't seem to distract what you had going with her. So, you obviously have a grip on that.

I have a grip on absolutely nothing.

No?

I wasn't doing anything.

Yes, well, that's good, maybe that's what it's all about. Maybe you could teach the rest of us to do that.

If I were doing something, then I could teach you how to do what I was doing.

You could teach us to do nothing. If that's what you were doing...nothing.

But I was not doing nothing. Nothing was being done.

I'm in agreement with that.

So if nothing is being done, then how does one teach this nothing?

Then people have to quit doing.

Okay. So quit it! You've heard it. You've heard what is a clear path.

Mm, I think...

Pay attention! You haven't been paying attention. That's your problem! *(laughter)*

I think if we were content, in the moment...

Mmhm?

...then we would quit trying to satisfy ourselves with other distractions.

Ab-sol-utely! *If* you were content, you would be content.

So, basically the chore for us is just to enjoy nothing. When we can enjoy nothing then everything else is sort of like...how do you say it...icing on the cake.

Quite a chore to enjoy nothing.

And I'm enjoying the icing on the cake, but if there's no icing I still enjoy the cake.

Then you are blessed.

♋   ♋   ♋

STAYING WITH THE I AM

It seems like teachers recommend to stay with the 'I Am' as long as possible.

Like you really have to recommend that to people! *(laughing)* Once you have known that, you say, "I want that again." You don't have to have some teacher recommend that you get back there, you'll want it with your entire being.

I find the urge to be in the 'I Am' happens a lot.

So, that is what occurs to you: "I think I am going to try to get back in the 'I Am.'" This is not a mainstream kind of thought. This is not what the average guy on the street is trying to do. This is an activity that is somewhat unique and is found only in seeker body-mind mechanisms, of which there are relatively few. And those particular body-mind mechanisms have been created and constructed and programmed in such a way that what comes to their mind is, "I think I want to try to get into the 'I Am' state," rather than, "I want to get tickets to the opera or tickets to the ballgame." So your form of entertainment is different.

Well, you could remind yourself, couldn't you? You can be constantly putting little reminders around the house, "I AM NOT THE DOER." When you are getting up in the morning, perhaps a notice on the wall. You know, constantly remind yourself. How about that?

Little refrigerator magnets, "I am not the doer"? You've got quite a potential enterprise going there. But whether or not you see those reminders, and whether or not the seeing of those reminders activates some sense of non-doership, is not in your control.

♋   ♋   ♋

LIFE IS DISTRACTING

It's tricky though. Real tricky.

What's tricky?

It's so distracting.

What's distracting?

Life is distracting. There's so much going on.

Distracting from what?

Well, that's it. It's distracting from life. So, that's confusing. But it seems true.

What I really love is the statement, "You have to still the mind." (laughs) You want your mind still? I'll still your mind. I'll hit you with this chair, you'll have a still mind. *(laughs)* I mean, what's the big deal? You want to be out? I can get you out. I can give you a fifth of scotch and have you drink it in half an hour. You'll be out! I can give you a little ether, a little too much valium. You'll be out! You want out, you can get out. That's not a problem!

*Then why is it that so many teachers say silence is
where you know what's going on?*

Because most are simply repeating what someone
else said. They don't KNOW! But the teacher who knows,
knows that the silence is not *phenomenal* silence! It is a
transcendence of that.

So, it doesn't have anything to do with the mind?

Nothing! This body-mind is an instrument. It works
the way it does because that's the way it's designed! Now,
the first sage who suggested that a disciple try to still his
mind, probably did so, so that the disciple could see the
futility of it. Thus, in that process of attempting to do
that there could be some kind of transcendent movement,
a seeing that this was not possible. There is a seeing that
that which was trying to still the mind, couldn't still the
mind. You see? In that moment, in that instant, with
that sage, this may have been an extraordinarily potent
teaching tool. And then the next fellow who came after
him in the lineage (who didn't have any understanding
at all) could only say, "Sit and still the mind. You must
still the mind." And that, too, is part of the functioning
of Totality. That they said that is part of the dance as well.

*But the mind is what causes all the suffering. The
way the mind is seeing things causes all this suffering. I
don't know, I think I should stop thinking.*

Okay. (laughs) I'm not stopping you.

I don't think it's possible.

No, it's not possible. It happens. There are points at
which your involvement in this thinking process stops.
The thinking process is purely a process of the brain. That
is what the brain does. As long as the brain has oxygen
going to it, and nerves associated with it, it's going to do

that. Just like the heart is going to pump, the brain is going to process thoughts!

Oh! There are reports of people who go into samadhi for long periods, but it seems they can't be there all the time and be functioning in the world because they just stop. To walk around, they have to come back to normal consciousness. So, it seems that you need this 'me' to function in the world.

But *samadhi* is not Awakening! It is a phenomenal state, in which consciousness of the personal self is absent. That can be induced with drugs. I can hit you over the head with a bat and simulate that experience. So what?!

Well, what I was thinking of was people like Ramana Maharshi. They have photographs of him sitting there, and sometimes he would just spontaneously go into some state, right?

Sure! But lots of yogis do that. The fact that one in which there was Understanding did that, doesn't have so much to do with the Understanding itself, as of the 'spiritual context' of that body-mind mechanism in which those kinds of states happen.

♋   ♋   ♋

FREE SAMPLES

There are glimpses of that Oneness. Are the glimpses the same as when Enlightenment happens?

No, they are similar. The glimpse that you have is the glimpse that one gets from total disidentification. What happens is that there are states where there is no *you* present, but when there is no *you* present, there is no *you* present to experience that state. The experience of the *no-you* being present comes about afterwards. So you say, "I had this experience." But that *experience* was actually your absence. When your relative presence returns, it gives that space of absence qualities, based on its background and its spiritual culture. The glimpse itself has no quality. It is not knowable by a me.

It is a wonderful experience, though.

But what I'm suggesting is that while that is happening, there is no EXPERIENCE. Because there is no *experiencer*.

Non-duality.

It is non-duality which is the default state. This notion of bliss (this notion of the absence of problems) is the overlay that comes about subsequent to it. And that's why people from varying cultures, different times, different religious backgrounds will describe this in different terms, because the overlay that is put on it, is the one of their own conditioning. It is expressed through that conditioning, as an experience of that body-mind mechanism which has various qualities and characteristics. But the *experience* itself, or the absence of the experiencer, is the absence of any body-mind mechanism to experience anything.

But the glimpse is equivalent, is it not, to a non-dual life or whatever term we have to use for it. It's either permanent or impermanent. But it's the same, true?

No. Because in the glimpse that you have, the only way that you know you have a glimpse is to bring it into phenomenality.

As a comparison, you're saying? Of what it is not?

As something with qualities! In duality.

Then how do you know that you are in this all the time?

That is the wonderful paradox. If you 'know' you are in it...you aren't!

Okay.

It is precisely what the sages have been saying from day one...nothing happens! No *one* is enlightened. Any experience of understanding happens to a *me*, and no me can ever be enlightened. All experiences are in phenomenality.

And turning it into an experience is already the separation from it?

Yes! To know something, to experience something, it has to be quantified. This experience of Oneness or Union that you have most assuredly had is actually *your* absence. It is the absence of a *you* to take delivery of the experience. It is only when *you* re-emerge that this absence ends. *You* are the beginning and ending brackets to the absence. Once bracketed, the absence is then quantified as some*thing*, an event, an experience.

For the sage, there is no ending bracket. The sense of a personal *me* does not return to bracket the absence and make it knowable. Thus, it can be said that the sage does not know that he is enlightened.

An American sage, Robert Adams, once suggested that we have an "Enlightened Beings" convention and that anyone who showed up would be immediately disqualified. *(laughter)*

Can there be experiencing with no me ?

There can be Experiencing, without an experiencer. A capital 'E,' Experiencing. But it doesn't have any of the qualities of experiencing with a small 'e.' It is simply another word for ultimate Understanding, for being the Oneness.

Many of the sages I've read about talk about the state of awareness of the Self as being a state of Bliss.

Yes, but you know what? Not one of them spoke English. Well, okay—*rarely* in history have we found someone using the term 'bliss' from an original sampling rather than a translation of the Sanskrit word *ananda*. Right?

Yeah. (laughter)

And the problem with the term 'bliss' is that it conjures up this notion of incredible goodness and wonderfulness without any counterbalancing negativity. What it suggests is that you can have a one-ended stick. The Bliss that the sages talk about is a transcendent state. It is an encompassing of the duality such that the states of pleasure and pain, happiness and sadness, good and bad—all of these things are encapsulated. The dilemma, the paradox, is not solved, it is dissolved. And that Understanding is the Bliss that the sages talk about. It has nothing to do with the phenomenal experience that the word *bliss* conjures up, which is the conditioned opposite of misery. That is not the state that the sages are talking about.

Typically the seeker thinks of Understanding in individual terms. He or she thinks of Enlightenment as something which will happen to *me*. "And when *I'm* enlightened, then *I'm* not going to have any problems. I'm not going to care whether or not my bills get paid. I'm not going to care whether my commitments get met. I'll just live footloose and fancy-free and everything's going to be taken care of." Well, the understanding is that everything is being taken care of. But the problems and

bills continue, the inability to satisfy everyone continues, all of those things which frustrate the body-mind
mechanism continue within phenomenality, because the
individual is *not enlightened.* Enlightenment is an impersonal state. It is a Transcendent Understanding.

It cannot exist in a body-mind organism?

It is not *limited* to the body-mind organism. The
body-mind organism is merely an aspect of the Totality.
What falls away is the sense of personal doership, the
sense that *I* am the one—as a limited *me*—who is performing particular actions. The Understanding is that it
is all a unified whole. But that isn't an understanding
which is held by an individual mind. The individual
doesn't know that. Understanding is Transcendent. Understanding is What Is.

♋   ♋   ♋

UP THE PENDULUM
AND DOWN AGAIN

*Wayne, one night after your talk, I woke up in the
middle of the night, and there were no thoughts, and I
was experiencing every moment. It was so enjoyable and
wondrous. Wondrous. To just experience nothing. The mind
was totally quiet. No thoughts at all. And then occasionally I could feel a thought start to arise, but then it would
just go away. And this lasted probably for an hour. Then
I went to sleep, and when I woke up my mind was going
'ding-ding, ding-ding-ding, ding-ding, ding-ding-ding.'
I thought, "Oh shucks, here it is, doing its little tricks,
its little chattering." And the computer had turned back
on again.*

So, what you're describing is this movement up to the very top of the pendulum shaft, in which all this life stuff is not associated with this body-mind mechanism. That it's all somehow not connected, which is a very freeing kind of feeling. Because in that moment there's no attachment, and thus there's no suffering. So, this is all going on, but it's not going on in any way that affects you. Then it changed back into involvement.

Well, through the last thirty years of my seeking I've had a lot of experiences of bliss and being out of my body, and looking down at the world...and I always thought that these were signs of getting somewhere. (laughter)

Yes, you got somewhere...you did get somewhere. There! You got there! *(laughter)*

But the experience of no-mind was...

Is Here!

...was by far the more...it was just much more...even though it wasn't grandiose, it was more of an experience of reality.

I always hate to be the party-pooper in these things...

I know. I know. (laughter)

But this is still an experience in phenomenality! Even that wondrous sense of total non-separation that one experiences at the top of the pendulum. That sense of absolute ease and being in comfort with all that is, is still a phenomenal experience. It is still located in an individual. And that is why it is transient!

But there was no mind there. There was no functioning mind there.

There was no sense of personal doership there.

Right.

I understand. But there is still a locus of awareness, if you will, that was associated with a separate body-mind organism. As opposed to the final dissolution which is the merging of that sense, that point of identification with the Infinite.

So, if I had already merged with the Infinite, then I wouldn't have had that experience?

That is correct.

So, there would have been no me there...

To have that experience.

Oh! (laughter) But that was the fun of it!

Yes, it is more exciting to be the seeker than the sought.

But I've heard you say that when you've merged, there's still joy, and you're having wonderful experiences, but not as a person.

That's the thing. The body-mind mechanism experiences all of the emotions and responses that are a part of the nature of the organism. But there is no *me* there to get *involved* with them

♋   ♋   ♋

TEMPORARY ENLIGHTENMENT?

Are there ever glimpses of the merging and then coming back? I've heard other enlightened teachers, or supposed enlightened teachers say that you can come back out of it.

*You can become enlightened but then you can come back
out of it.*

No. What you can come back out of is the state that
you described. That is the state where all these people
go and set up shop.

You mean they're up there permanently?

They're up there at the top of the pendulum shaft
saying, "This is my experience." And they'll say, "Yes,
and we can fall out of that, back into identification, and
then go back into that experience again." But that is not
the Awakening that the sages talk about. And the transient experience is not uncommon. You hear this within
certain, what I like to think of as, multi-level marketing
schemes for spirituality. *(laughter)* You have someone
who's had an experience of Oneness, who says, "Look,
this is available to you! You can awaken! You can have
this experience! Do what I did and you'll get this result."
So, these people do what he did, they get this result, they
have this sense of bliss, of not being involved with their
thoughts, and they go, *(slap)* "Okay, I'm awakened! Now
I'm going to teach you." And then he gets eight people
under him, and then they *awaken*. Now you have this
tremendous wave of *awakening* that's going on. And the
great guru up here that has helped all of these people
awaken is seen as a very wonderful, very fine, very profound, strong guru. And all of his sub-gurus, down
through this pyramid, are funneling disciples up through
the pyramid and...*(laughter)* You can see it in action. It's
a new spiritual movement. You don't have to look very
far! *(laughter)*

Nearly every seeker has had the experience of being at the very top of the pendulum shaft—I'm sure you
have, if you've been a seeker for a while. You feel that
you are one with everything and no longer affected by

anything. Everything is simply happening, and you are simply the witness of it. You're not involved in it, it's just going on, and it doesn't matter. There are a number of names for this mystical union, which is an impersonal connection with the very nature of existence. It is the absence of any*one* to be involved with any*thing*. It is your relative absence as the doer.

So if this happens to *you*, you're very likely to think, "I have done something to get here. Let's see, what was the last thing I did? Well, I went to that seminar, I practiced that meditation..." And so you double your efforts to either get *back* to the top of the pendulum shaft, or to *stay* there! If you are lucky enough to be at the top for a period of time, you might start to think, "I've got this deal. This is what all the sages have been talking about, right? I'm witnessing! I've read Maharaj, 'you've got to be the witness'! And, I'm doing that! I am there. I Am That! What could be better? I can do my own seminars! People will come to hear me! This'll be great!"

So you put up your shingle and begin giving satsang. The problem is that this point at the top of the pendulum is still a point in phenomenality, it is still a point of *experience*, albeit impersonal experience, and as such it is subject to change. Everything in phenomenality changes. Therefore, at some point, when something happens such as being diagnosed with cancer or someone close to you dying—there is a *realization* that the pendulum shaft is *greased*, and you're sliding back down again for *the big swing*. *(laughter)* At this point the intensity of your feelings of dejection are *double* what they were previously, because you feel as if you've lost something *terribly* important, that you've lost your union with God or the Infinite, that you've *fallen from Grace*. Now you're back to being involved and swinging with all the other plebes, when before, you and God were like *this!* *(Holds up two fingers crossed, laughter)*

Now, if you've put out your shingle and you've told everybody, "*It happened* to me! *I'm* the guy!" *(laughter)*, then you're *triply* screwed because you either have to come clean and say, "Um...I *thought* I was enlightened, but...it was sort of a false alarm. Sorry about that." *Or* you have to begin living a lie, which is not a fun thing to have to do. And actually there is a third option that is gaining in popularity...you can redefine Enlightenment to *include* the flip-flop. You say, "I am Enlightened, but I am *stabilizing* into the experience." But when Enlightenment actually happens there is no longer anyone to stabilize or be delivered into anything!

What is important to understand is that what the sages are talking about is not a movement from identification to disidentification within phenomenality. It is a total quantum movement from identification with the entire pendulum shaft of phenomenality to identification with the fulcrum upon which the pendulum depends.

The state in which there is identification at the fulcrum, is utter, complete, quantum eradication of the sense of personal doership, of that which gets involved with the movement. Then there is simply pure Beingness, which is not a change in anything. That is What Is, That is already here, That is the *state* that eternally exists. In That there can be no flip-flop.

Another important thing to remember about the fulcrum is that nothing happens there. All movement, all action, happens around the fulcrum, yet the fulcrum is completely unmoved by everything. Therefore, it is not that the sage is witnessing something, rather, in the most profound sense, the sage *is* everything. As such, there is no experience associated with that. All experience is within a subject-object relationship within phenomenality. The movement to Ultimate Understanding, or that identification with the Totality that is called Enlightenment, is a movement in which *nothing happens*. That is why

Ramesh is so fond of saying, "If you have the choice between getting Enlightenment or getting a million dollars,
take the million dollars! Because if you get the million
dollars, there will be *someone* there to enjoy it, but if Enlightenment comes, there won't be *anyone* there to enjoy
anything!"

A friend of mine called me a number of years ago
from Hawaii. He had been going to a teacher who was
describing this experience of oneness as being Enlightenment, and one day he got it! And he called me to tell
me he had woken up. And he was describing this to me,
and how, "It hasn't gone away, and it's been a couple of
days, and everything has a new light, and it looks different," and how he's, "One with all of this." And I'm
listening to him and my heart sinks and I'm thinking,
"Oh, man...*(laughter)*...not you!" And it was probably a
year, or a year and a half after that he tried to kill himself.

*So, he experienced so much freedom, and then to go
back into the garbage again was too devastating to him?*

Mmhm.

How long did it last for him?

I don't know. I never talked to him about the details. It wasn't important, really. Nor did I, at the time,
have the heart to tell him that this wasn't IT either. That
what he was describing was a wonderful, fabulous, life
experience, but an experience within phenomenality
which *will* eventually end. I can assure you, people do
not appreciate being told this.

*How do you know the difference? Do you have to
have somebody tell you?*

No.

Then you just know the difference?

Yes. When it happens there's no question. There's no-one for whom the question occurs. The whole thing is over. All of the questions are gone.

And you can't go back?

There is no *me* left to go back. What is left is What Is. Phenomenally speaking, all those wonderful, get-away-from-it-all kinds of feelings that are associated with not being involved with the body-mind mechanism...those go, too. There's no one to experience that either. There are simply the direct responses of the body-mind mechanism. That is all that's left.

So, from the outside, to the casual observer, usually there is no apparent dramatic change that happens as a result of this so-called Awakening. The body-mind mechanism continues on essentially as it has. In some cases, that body-mind mechanism may then take on the role of a teacher. But certainly not necessarily. And if it takes on the role of a teacher, then, various other kinds of trappings tend to go along with it. These can get projected by others, depending on the tradition that the teaching is in. But as far as the Teacher is concerned, there is no individual there to be concerned.

Did you live at the top of the pendulum for awhile before Awakening occurred?

Oh, I had my moments there, sure.

It wasn't like a stationary state for awhile?

Not for any significant period of time, no—which is both a blessing and a curse. Those people who had that experience for long periods—say weeks or months...

Or a sort of a stable state?

It's not a stable state. In phenomenality, it's an unstable state. When you come out of it—which you inevitably do—then the *crash* after you've been there for awhile is just awesome.

Did you notice a diminution of seeking before the Awakening occurred for you, or did it happen just overnight?

There was a period where the intellectual understanding had taken root, if you will, to the extent that I just felt more ease and comfort and peace walking around in my own skin.

Would you say that some kind of shifting occurred?

Sure. I would say that the shift was a deepening of the understanding. Now, I wouldn't particularly connect that with the impersonal Awakening. That would be like comparing apples and oranges. They are different.

Because that's still within the realm of experiencing?

Exactly. The advantage of intellectual understanding from the personal standpoint is that it makes life easier. As the intellectual understanding deepens, as there is the recognition that Consciousness is the doer and then the sense of personal doership diminishes, ultimately, there is more ease and comfort in being alive.

A lot of the struggle goes?

A lot of the struggle goes. Now, I would go so far as to say that for someone looking at this body-mind mechanism from outside and evaluating its actions, it would appear that there was much more peace during that period before the so-called Awakening happened. I was 'mellower.' Afterwards, there was no filter whatsoever on what was happening. There was no longer the gauze of intellectual understanding to mitigate the reactions in the body-mind mechanism and its nature, as there was previously. All the character defects and associated qualities which are inherent in the mechanism were no longer being 'toned down' as they had been by the intellectual understanding.

And then...?

And now the body-mind mechanism just does what the body-mind mechanism does, in accordance with its nature, and there isn't any secondary involvement. Some people meet me, experience Resonance and call me a guru. Others meet me, have some other kind of experience with me, and call me an asshole. And so it goes.

♋   ♋   ♋

THE FLIP FLOP

Ramesh talked about the 'flip-flop.' Could you talk a bit about that? Is that something you experience?

Any flip-flop is experiential. Any flip-flop is a movement in and out of relative understanding. It is a movement from the top of the pendulum, back down the pendulum shaft. There is no flip-flop from the pendulum to the fulcrum. Once you're a pickle, you are not a cucumber anymore. And there is no going back to cucumberhood.

I have had the experience of being beyond knowing and not knowing, but now I seem to be lost.

But you can only be lost if you are trying to get somewhere.

There are moments when I'm lost and then I'm not lost, there is searching and then I'm in the moment.

So, when the acceptance comes, the acceptance brings you back here, into the eternal Present Moment, in which there is no possibility of being lost. All the goals, all the aspirations, all the desires are out there. Here is where life is. Here is where the peace is.

You know, I'm sitting here trying to figure things out. It seems like it doesn't really matter what you're doing, that it's more up to whatever Grace feels like doing.

Grace is the operative principle. That is what is doing the doing.

I guess I'm not thinking in terms of still being involved in Divine Hypnotism, but as long as you're still thinking and trying to figure things out from that angle, you're still in the losing mode as far as trying to get where you want to be. (laughs)

You're *always* in the 'losing mode' in terms of trying to get where you want to be, because where you want to go doesn't exist. There is no place other than Here.

The Divine Hypnosis is tricky. Sometimes you can sit there and accept all of it, but then at other times, without even realizing it, you're right back to being totally caught up in it. But since the doer fell off of you, Wayne, the difference between us is that you don't get caught back up in that hypnotism anymore, right?

Yes, the Divine Hypnosis is gone.

So, things are happening, but there's no one taking possession of them anymore?

Right. No involvement as a separate 'doer.'

It's too bad that drugs can't 'get you there.' (laughter) They don't get you where you really want to be.

No, the drugs don't *get you there*, they can only get you to a point where the Divine Hypnosis is seen through. When you hit that point on a good acid trip or some other good hallucinogen high, where you are in that state of oneness...that is the *experience* of non-separation. You can say it's an impersonal experience, but it's still an experience, and as such, it's temporary. And what is talked about as the state of *Enlightenment* is not temporary, is not by its nature even phenomenal. It is that which is transcendent of the entire phenomenal manifestation. It is that which the entire phenomenal world arises out of. You can call it God, or you can call it Consciousness, or you can call it Tao, or Source, or Oneness, or Totality, or whatever—it doesn't matter what you call it—but That is all there is, and all of *this* is simply an aspect of That.

In a good meditation, when thought has pretty much stopped, it would seem that maybe the hypnosis hasn't stopped, but that it has been lessened a bit at that point. Or is that just another part of the hypnosis?

Another part of the hypnosis.

It's the quiet part of the hypnosis. (laughs)

Yes, as long as there is the knowledge that *"I'm* quiet."

Yes, there's always that.

♋   ♋   ♋

I AM THAT,
BUT I KEEP FORGETTING

I know that what I really am is fulfillment itself, what I am is that absolute perfection. I know that in my deepest experience, but it doesn't translate into twenty-four-hour-a-day realization.

Now when you say that you're that perfection, what do you mean by that?

I was referring to my meditation experiences. It doesn't have to be during meditation, but it seems to be correlated to meditation. That's when I get the experience of Aham Brahmasmi: "I am this universe; this whole universe is my Self. There's nothing to be lost or gained. I don't live, I don't die; I am that self-sufficient perfection." I do have that experience. And then when I read the Ashtavakra Gita, I think: "Aha perfect. Reflecting on this is vibrating absolutely perfectly with my state of consciousness, and it's wonderful. I am That." But then I go about my business, and apparently the knowing is not fixed. It's just a discreet experience like everything else. Then I know that that's not it, so my mind is constantly churning, discerning, and discriminating, remembering, and texturing, and wanting to get at that Ultimate Ground. That's a constant activity. It's not even 'me,' it's just a process going on. I can't claim credit for anything, I'm just using everything in the environment available to try and get at that essence of who I am.

And you are absolutely correct: it is a process, and it is not your process.

I would agree with that.

It is very much the play of Consciousness that is operating through you, so that all of these actions, all of these thoughts, all of these experiences happen through this body-mind mechanism. And what you know as that perfection, that Oneness, is your relative absence.

True. When I hear about this state of non-being or no personal self, intellectually, it's terrifying. But when I've experienced that, I felt, "Wow, what a relief! There's no personality, no bodily identification, 'I' don't exist, how wonderful!"

But actually that experience of delight that you have is simply the flip side of the coin of the experience of fear.

That's my next point. There hasn't been a time when I experienced bliss that I didn't also experience some degree of discomfort afterwards whether it's rage, or doubt, or fear. Usually it's anger, some kind of bodily or psychic reaction to the tremendous expansion of consciousness. It's fifty-fifty. However great the bliss was, that's how great the disturbance will be every time without fail.

Yes, the 'pendulum' swings. It happens, and my point in all of this is that the experience of oneness and the experience of fear are both experiences. It is just that one seems to be very spiritual in nature while the other appears to be unspiritual. But they are not different. It's a very common misconception that this experiential state of oneness is somehow different in its fundamental character from the experience of fear and separation. Both are experiences in phenomenality, both are overlays onto What Is. The What Is, in fact, has no separate quality of either fear or bliss. The ultimate state of Understanding encompasses both and absorbs both, but is neither to the exclusion of the other.

Ꮼ   Ꮼ   Ꮼ

THE CESSATION
OF QUESTIONS

Once there is an understanding of this, then in a way it kind of seems ridiculous to ask questions. Like you said, all there is is Consciousness, Consciousness is all there is. And it seems like I'm just entertaining the mind in asking all these questions.

Once the Understanding is complete there are no more questions. It isn't that the sage has all the answers, the sage just doesn't have any more questions.

How come my body temperature goes up so much when I sit here and listen to you talk?

Does it matter?

I suppose not. It just happens—one can look at it that way and accept that as What Is, just as everything else can be accepted as What Is.

Up to and including the question, "Why?"—that is also part of What Is.

So, there is no ,"Why?" for anything?

Oh, there are *thousands* of "Whys" for *everything*! That's the *problem* ! Take your pick! *(laughter)* As soon as you get the answer to one question, it will spawn two more. Which reminds me of a story...

Years ago there was an island surrounded by a reef and the reef was being attacked and slowly eaten by starfish. So, the islanders (who were completely dependent on the reef for food) got together and went out to solve the problem. They dove down and plucked the starfish off the reef and then threw them up into the boats. In the boat was a guy with a machete who would cut the starfish in half and then throw the pieces overboard.

(laughter) The people laughing know that starfish regenerate. Each half of the cut-up starfish would then grow into a fully whole starfish. Soon there were twice as many starfish. Questions are like that too. And sometimes I get to play the somewhat ludicrous role of the guy with the machete.

I guess that's the beauty of being in the moment. Questions don't even come up then.

That's right. Now armed with that little piece of information, the usual and logical reaction to that is, "Okay, I'm just going to shut up. I'm not going to appear unenlightened here. The more questions I ask, the more clear it is that I missed the point. Therefore, I'll just stop asking questions." Then you can walk around with an insipid New Age grin on your face saying, "I don't have any more questions left." *(laughter)* But it is when the questions *stop*—something over which you have no control whatsoever—that the peace comes. To have the questions arise and simply push them down and not ask them doesn't get you anywhere.

I find that questions arise while I'm driving here or the day before, yet it seems like they get answered without my having to ask you.

I appreciate that, it saves me a lot of work. *(laughter)*

In fact, sometimes the answers are so obvious that I think, "Why does that question even come up?" But then again, why ask the, "Why," it just comes up.

Perhaps somebody else needs to hear the answer to that question, but they don't have the courage to ask.

Good point, yes.

Everything that happens could not have happened any other way and can be explained in many ways. Or as Ram Tzu put it, "Nothing is unexplainable. Everything is a mystery."

♋   ♋   ♋

GIVING UP THE SEARCH

I've tried different things and read alternative books and seen a lot of different teachers. And I'm still searching. Still searching, but getting less intense in my outward efforts. I'm almost ready to give up meditation, actually. I'm even ready to give up reading Ashtavakra Gita! I'm really kind of at that point.

Well, we'll see if those things are ready to give you up! *(laughter)* Because until they're ready to give you up, your opinion on whether you're ready to give them up is irrelevant. It's only when your decision to give them up coincides with their decision to give you up that they disappear.

Hmm. So they're real friends, huh?

Perhaps.

I never thought of it that way.

The presumption involved in saying, "I think I'm about ready to give this up," is that *you* have some position on which to stand to effect that kind of change, that *you* have some sort of power that you can exercise to create that change in your life. And I'm sure you've often experienced that in your life, where you've made decisions such as "Okay *(smacks tabletop)* goddamn it, I am not going to do this for another day. I have decided I am going to give this up!" Yet, you find yourself continuing to do that thing despite the fact that you have decided to give it up. It has not given you up, therefore it keeps happening. Now what we say in those situations is, "I just didn't want to give that up badly enough. If I had really, in my heart of hearts, wanted to give it up, it would be gone."

I did that once. I gave up smoking.

Yes, as I said, when the confluence of the two is such that it gives you up at the same time as you give it up, then there's every appearance that you have got some kind of control. And you will use that one example to sustain the notion that you have some kind of power, despite ten other examples to the contrary.

♋   ♋   ♋

SEEKING HAS BECOME MY LIFE

I realized the other night that in my quest for deeper understanding, basically all that was, was a 'doing,' and since that quest is what propelled me as a seeker, it was like I had to give up what makes me a seeker. I mean, when you give up that quest for deeper understanding, it seems in a way like the seeking comes to a halt.

But who is there to give that up?

It's just an understanding in Consciousness coming through here that there's nothing really to seek anyway, because there's no 'me.'

The seeking happened. It will happen through the body-mind mechanism as long as it is in the *interest* of Totality, for the seeking to happen. And it will likewise cease at such time and place as Totality decides. Even that is a movement in Consciousness. Even the impulse or the thought that, "I am the seeker and I have to stop the seeking," is part of the whole dance.

You slowed me down for a moment.

Good.

I think we should just stop looking.

Alright, that's fine with *me*. I won't stop you. *(laughter)*

And looking for what? There's nothing to look for. I know that intellectually, but why does the body keep doing things to seek?

Because it's still a body-mind mechanism through which seeking happens.

Alright, will the seeking stop only when complete understanding occurs?

Only when the time comes for the seeking to stop and not one moment earlier. And the seeking can stop before there is ultimate Understanding.

It can?

Of course it can. When you just say, "To hell with it. I've had enough of this. I'm going to watch football on TV. *(laughter)* I'm going to do something important for a change." And then it happens.

The thought of giving up seeking is also kind of scary. Seeking has become my pastime, my whole life. If I had to give up seeking, I'd have to give up my main activity and I'd be lonely.

Perhaps, although I think there are lots of other people out there pursuing lots of activities other than seeking who aren't lonely. There are people who have found sympathetic groups who are interested in drag racing or professional football or crocheting or whatever, and they have clubs and meet and exchange information and have social interactions around that interest. Maybe your interest in attaining union with God will be replaced by crocheting. *(laughter)* And you'll find a whole new group of people to associate with and explore your *inner crocheter.* Anything is possible.

Anything is possible.

Of course that would probably play hell with your self-image! As a *seeker after Truth,* one tends to hold oneself in rather high regard. *(laughter)*

♋　　♋　　♋

I MUST BE DOING IT WRONG

Ramesh is questioned about this a lot in Consciousness Speaks, and he says that if there's any sign, or any state prior to Enlightenment, it would be that you just don't care either way.

I know, and you will now see some of the people around Ramesh who have been there for a while, saying, "Oh, I don't care!" *(laughter)* "Oh, I don't care about Enlightenment. Oh, no, no, not me, I'm way past caring about Enlightenment."

Yeah. (laughter)

Then what are you doing here you fool?! You're in goddamn Bombay, of all places. You haven't had a solid shit in six months and you are covered with bedbug bites! Don't tell me you don't care! *(laughter)* I mean, if you didn't care, you'd be on Maui! Yes, it really is ridiculous.

In the world, if you study any subject, like French for thirty years, (like I've been involved in "The Search") you'd be pretty good at it by then. You'd regard yourself as a French scholar. But with this sort of work, you cannot, and you get to a point where you just feel you've got to give up! You've got to let go...

If you're lucky! *(laughter)* A lot of people have been at it a lot longer than thirty years without having given it up! And they consider themselves quite knowledgeable on the subject.

Sure. But underlying that, there is still that sense of frustration, wanting to go home, and not getting there. So, there's that conundrum, shall I lead just an everyday, in-the-moment life, but still wanting this deep bliss, or whatever you would call it?

Yes! It is very much the frustration of the fish in the ocean, searching for water.

Yes. So...(laughter)

So?

Can you tell me what I'm doing wrong?

What on earth makes you think you're doing something wrong? Or that you could do anything other than what you've done? The presumption being, of course, that *you're doing* it! That's certainly a reasonable assumption. All of your experience would suggest that that is the case, as long as it's not looked at very closely *(laughs)*. There is a sense of personal doership there. So, as long as that sense of personal doership is there, there will be a feeling that you're doing it, and that if you haven't gotten to where you want to go, then the only logical conclusion is that you haven't done it very well. And that would lead to frustration, wouldn't it? Lord knows, you've tried hard enough. You've been as earnest and diligent as you possibly could be, and if you haven't gotten it BY NOW, you must be a consummate screw-up! *(laughter)* It's the only reasonable conclusion. Or, there's the unreasonable conclusion, which is that *you aren't doing it*, and that everything that's been done through that body-mind mechanism could not have been otherwise.

So, I might as well stop trying.

You are not doing the trying. You cannot stop the trying or affect the trying in any way!

But sometimes I get so impatient!

Yes! That's true. Sometimes you get impatient. Impatience comes.

And yet, I know I have no choice, and sometimes that's comforting.

Of course. Knowing that you have no choice, at the intellectual level, can bring about a certain degree of comfort, as you remind yourself intellectually that this is all happening perfectly. It is all happening precisely as it is supposed to be happening. It could not be happening any other way. There is nothing whatsoever that you could do differently. There's amazing comfort in that.

♋   ♋   ♋

GIVING UP

So a person can't say, "Okay, I'm going to give up. I'm just going to be That."

Wouldn't you have done it by now if you could have?

I just want to hear you say it. (laughter)

Of course you would have. Everybody in this room would have.

Just like we don't have a choice about being here at this very moment with you, right?

Correct. You just didn't get a better offer. *(laughter)*

♋   ♋   ♋

Anyone who has ever "gotten it" by following some
so-called method, has gotten it in spite of the method,
not because of it.

Lee Lozowick

One sees it as marvelous, another also speaks of it as
marvelous, but even after having heard of it, no one
whatsoever knows it.

Bhagavad Gita

One has not understood until one has forgotten it.

Suzuki Daisetz

Just because everything is different
doesn't mean anything has changed.

Irene Poter

Where did the truth go? The key was mislaid in an
army of doors, it was there on its ring with the others,
but the lock is nowhere in the world. No world for the
key to get lost in, no true or false, in the end.

Pablo Neruda

Just when I found out the meaning of life,
they changed it.

George Carlin

You equate serenity with mildness.
You prefer your Masters
Be nearly comatose,
Or better yet - Dead.
Enlightenment is not
A means of escape.
Everyone has problems.

Ram Tzu knows this:
Jesus being nailed to the cross
Knew he was having a bad day.

Problems are not problems at all,
but results that are dissatisfying.
Jerry Gillis

Ram Tzu's contentment
Has nothing to do
With his happiness
Or unhappiness

Even to be attached to the idea of Enlightenment is to
go astray.
Sengtsan, Third Zen Patriarch

Nobody gets in to see the wizard.
Not no way, not no how.
Wizard of Oz

SIX

ENLIGHTENMENT

WHO'S ENLIGHTENED?

Ramesh was asked in one of his books if he had received complete Grace. Not in that language, but basically he was asked, "Are you enlightened?" And for the purposes of who or what asked the question he said, "Yes."

I would ask you the same question. Your body-mind mechanism, has it received that Grace?

There is Understanding here.

Well, I have understanding here.

That's not the Understanding I'm talking about. *(laughter)*

That's what I'm asking.

And that is what I'm answering. That is my story and I'm sticking to it. *(laughter)*

၅   ၅   ၅

WAYNE'S STORY

Where was the body-mind mechanism when this event or whatever, happened?

When the 'nonevent' happened? *(laughter)*

...just curious, just curious.

Well, here's the story... *(laughter)* I was in love with two women, and when I returned from India after seeing Ramesh... this was in 1989... both women came to me in the same week and each told me she loved me very much but she was clearing the field for the other. And when the second one came to tell me that, I was enormously saddened.

There was some cause...?

No, this is the story. Pay close attention. You may have to do this. *(laughter)* So, when she came and told me that she was going to have to leave me, even though she loved me very much, I started to feel a real heaviness, a profound sadness come up in me. And I started to cry. And this sadness started to grow. And it kept growing. I found myself starting to cry harder, and this deep, deep sadness kept coming over me, like waves were crashing on me. And finally I found myself falling. It literally felt like I was falling into a pit, a horrible dark abyss of pain. And my body was racked with sobs. And it had ceased to have anything to do with anything fi-

nite. I was just free-falling into this pit of immense suffering... and it was growing blacker, and more painful,
and more horrendous by the second. I felt that I was
falling into this pit of suffering that was all of the suffering that has ever existed. And then there was a letting
go, a dissolution, a sense of merging, if you will, with
this suffering. And there was the certainty that nothing
could hurt me, because there was no *me* to hurt... there
was no separation any more. And the experience ebbed,
and I stopped crying, and I thought, somebody's going
to ask me about this, I better write this down. *(laughter)*
And yet, part of that knowing is exactly what I've been
saying all along... "literally, nothing happened." This
Understanding was there all along. What fell away was
an illusory veil, not something substantial. There was
nothing that was changed at all. All was exactly as it
always had been and ever would be. It was all perfect. It
all just Was.

69   69   69

WHAT IS ENLIGHTENMENT?

Would you say that the ego was annihilated?

I would say that the sense of personal doership was
annihilated. We're starting to get into terminology here,
but the reason I don't like to say that the ego was annihilated is because the way I usually use the word, the
ego is that collection of experiences and qualities that
make up the personality of a particular body-mind mechanism. That, obviously, is not gone in the case of a sage
or a jnani, or one in which there is Understanding. You
talk to him, he responds. He doesn't turn into a vegeta-
ble. His personality doesn't disappear. There is still an

ego in the sense that when you call his name, he responds. There is still a personality there. Therefore, I say that the ego is not gone. What is gone is the sense that that personality, the ego, is the doer. The locus of doership has shifted, from the individual, to the Whole.

I guess what I keep trying to imagine is, is Enlightenment something that is? Then I get an idea maybe that it is nothing that is. Is there someone in there, someone enjoying this whole thing of realizing that he is, "not the doer?"

Well, there is a body-mind mechanism that experiences. It enjoys some things and it doesn't enjoy others, just like every body-mind mechanism does, according to its conditioning. But there is no one there who is identified as the DOER. No one enjoying Enlightenment as an object.

If there is no doer, what do we have?

You have a mechanism in which there is no overlay of a sense of personal doership.

The mechanism, does it have sensations?

Of course. Of course, it has sensations as long as it is alive, as long as it is imbued with Consciousness. I mean, if it is in a coma, then it doesn't have any of those things.

There doesn't seem to be any central entity, central to all of this stuff, so is Ramesh, with a body-mind mechanism, aware that he is not the doer? And is he thinking, "It is just all happening."

There is no longer a Ramesh *with* a body-mind mechanism. There is only the body-mind mechanism with the name Ramesh. There is no separate Ramesh there to be aware that he is not the doer, or that the sense of personal doership is gone. The whole question is gone! The whole consideration of I'm the doer, I'm not the doer is gone! There is simply doing!

Is that true for everybody? Doing is just doing.

Doing is just doing. For most people there is a secondary quality of it being 'my' doing.

I see. The individual belongs to the mind-body mechanism so there isn't any individual when you get to the Ramesh stage. There is no individual there, right?

Well, again it depends on what you mean, because there is that aspect of the mechanism, that is differentiated as Ramesh, that responds and reacts in very Ramesh-like ways. There has been continuity throughout the span of that object that you can call the *Ramesh continuity*. An aspect of that Ramesh continuity is this impersonal event of Awakening or Enlightenment in which the sense of personal doership fell away, but the Ramesh character continues! There have been billions of actions and events that have happened through the Ramesh body-mind mechanism. Some actions are more interesting than others. We don't point to the eye-blink that happened on a certain date as being of any particular significance, but that eye blink, like Enlightenment was an event that happened through that body-mind mechanism. The significance is supplied afterwards.

Ramesh drove a car. There were literally millions of actions that could be said to be linked to his driving a car for 30 years through Bombay. Now, what all the repercussions and implications of those actions are, you can't begin to trace, and so they are not part of the history of that body-mind mechanism. All of the subsequent reactions and events that are not historically linked to that mechanism aren't known. Yet the web is incredible! The links are mind boggling! Literally so mind boggling that they cannot even begin to be comprehended. And ultimately everything is linked. Nothing is separate.

Did you recognize that there had been an under-standing when it happened to you?

Yes. I recognized that there had been an event, that the sense of personal doership, this thing that had seemed so real, had gone. Well, even to say that isn't correct. It's like this: you have a toothache, your entire perception of the world is viewed through the pain of that toothache. Everything is affected by that, and so your perceptions are the perceptions of one who has the toothache. You go to the dentist, he pulls the tooth, and you no longer have a toothache. In that instant you say, "Something's happened. My perception has shifted! I'm experiencing things now without that pain—what a tremendous re-lief! This is how the world REALLY IS." Two weeks later, you are not looking at the world through the absence of tooth pain. You are directly perceiving it as it is.

But there was something that happened to you.

Oh, there was an event, and it was dramatic, lots of crying and shaking and all kinds of excitement in that moment, but the understanding was, that this was just another event in phenomenality that happened through this body-mind mechanism, as part of the entire func-tioning of Totality—just like any other event.

After the realization happened did you stop actively seeking? Could you share with us a little more about that?

There was no one to seek.

I mean, prior to that, had you come to a place where you knew that actively seeking was futile... did you be-come still with the teaching?

Yes. There was a point where the intellectual understanding had deepened and there were really no longer any mental questions.

So, as long as we seek, as long as we're in the process of seeking, then that won't be final. Is that correct?

I would say that the seeking and the finding both fall away at the same instant. In the moment of Understanding, the whole conceptual framework, in which the seeker and the sought exist, dissolves.

♋   ♋   ♋

WHAT CHANGES
AFTER ENLIGHTENMENT?

When there is Understanding, is there some effect upon the organism?

There can be. It can have a variety of effects on the body-mind mechanism. I think the initial effect, or sensation, within the body, if you will, is beautifully described by Marc Beuret. He described it as putting down a heavy backpack. In the moment that you put down that pack, there is an intense feeling of relief associated with not carrying that pack. Very quickly, however, there is no sensation whatsoever of having *ever* carried the pack. You can remember that there was once a pack on your back. But you cannot really remember the feel of the weight.

It's no more a reference point at all?

Mmhm.

Like it never existed?

It never existed.

How old were you when you got this Understanding?

Thirty-eight. And what I would say is, literally nothing happened. In that moment of Understanding there was the recognition that nothing had happened. And that is one of the lovely paradoxes about this thing, and one of the reasons it's so damn hard to talk about. Because there is no one to become enlightened. No one in the entire history of the universe has ever been enlightened. And you're not going to be the first. *(laughter)*

This Understanding comes about in the absence of anyone to be enlightened, in the absence of anyone to know or understand anything.

Do you really not remember anything, or...

No, the problem is that you think in terms of an enlightened individual. You say this body-mind mechanism, this hunk of meat sitting here, is enlightened. And what I'm telling you is that this is a body-mind mechanism in the phenomenal dream-play, just like all of the rest of these body-mind mechanisms, with no difference in its inherent quality. It was born with certain genetic characteristics and it was born into a particular environment in which it was nurtured, and it had various experiences that gave it slightly different qualities and characteristics, so that it responds to things according to those characteristics. And it continues. Whether there is Understanding or not doesn't matter, because the Understanding has nothing to do with the mechanism. The Understanding is transcendent. When there is Understanding there is literally a falling away of the entire illusion. Now, it is impossible for the mind to conceive of Understanding without an understander. It's part of the limitations of language. Language always assumes a subject and an object. Our thinking is structured to operate in terms of subject-object relationship. The entire manifestation is in subject-object relationship. It is inconceivable, literally inconceivable, that there be something without subject-object relationship.

Yet, you have had tastes of it. And you've tasted it through an agency other than the mind. Because the mind is a splitting mechanism, a dividing mechanism. Whenever it is applied to anything it cuts it into pieces. Therefore, it cannot know the Whole. The moment it is applied to the Whole, it cuts it up!

♋   ♋   ♋

IS IT TRUE?

Is it true that...

No. *(loud laughter)* I'm sorry. Go ahead.

Is it true that fear and loneliness arise from the ego rather than from nature? Is it that when the ego vanishes there would be a change? I've got a question about fear and the sense of loneliness. When the ego finally vanishes, do these things vanish too?

Okay. You see, I make a very precise distinction between the sense of personal doership and the ego. And I do that for a specific reason. When the sense of personal doership disappears—the sense that *I am the doer*—there is still, within the body-mind mechanism, a structure which we would call the ego structure. The ego structure is that which knows it is Ramana Maharshi, such that when somebody calls out, "Ramana!" Ramana turns around. Without that ego structure there, Ramana doesn't know himself from Arunachala! *(loud laughter)*

Because it is all Consciousness. Right? So, the sense of personal doership has disappeared. There is no longer any sense that *I* am doing *anything*. But there is certainly a sense of presence as the body-mind mechanism that is associated, identified, as part of the body-mind mechanism. It is absolutely essential that it be there for functioning to happen. And you can say that this ego is the *person*-ality, where the *person* is associated with that body-mind mechanism. And that doesn't go. If it did, that body-mind mechanism wouldn't know what it ate, wouldn't have any memory, any culture. No learning. Nothing! So, what goes is the sense of personal doership—*not* the ego structure.

Does the sense of separate existence, which can feel alone and separate, have anything to do with the ego structure? Or is that to do with the doership?

There are aspects of the *person* which are associated with the sense of personal doership. Pride and guilt are directly connected with the sense of personal doership. If there is no sense of personal doership then there is no pride in doing! There is just action. There is no guilt about doing, there is simply action. So those are—out the window. *(roars with laughter with everyone)* The thing is, there's no one there *glad* that they're out the window! No one thinking, "Oh it is really great. I am so much better off now that they're not there." They are just *not* there.

So the ego doesn't disappear?

No.

So the ego doesn't think at all?

Now, this question about the ego, or the mind is why Ramesh, bless his heart, came up with the notion of the thinking mind and the working mind. *(laughter in room)* Now I REALLY HATE getting into this because it opens such a can of worms. I remember the day vividly. It was in Pennsylvania. He was doing a four-day retreat there. And out of the blue, he comes up with this concept of bifurcating the mind into the *working mind* and the *thinking mind.* The working mind is the operating aspect of the mind. The thinking mind is the aspect that gets involved in the working, that is synonymous with the sense of personal doership. The thinking mind is the one that worries about the results, and thus, inhibits the working of the working mind. He used that to try to point to what is *gone* when this sense of personal doership goes, because it is, of course, the question on everyone's mind. "What am I going to GET once I get this thing. What's it going to be like? How am I going to benefit when I finally attain this Enlightenment I have been searching for and seeking so desperately?" It is a question that comes up all the time.

So, he came up with this notion of the thinking mind and the working mind, and it was like throwing a piece of meat into a pack of ravening wolves. And that night the people were up past *two o'clock in the morning,* saying "Oh, is this the working mind or is this the thinking mind? If a pilot flies his plane into a mountain, *(claps hand)* what goes through the windshield first, is it the working mind or the thinking mind?" *(loud laughter)* It was INCREDIBLE! I've never seen anything like it in my life.

Do you still ever have, at any time, a sense of I Am?

No, all of those are movements in phenomenality that are connected to a sense of personal doership. Even with an impersonal sense of doership, if you will, which is what is often described as the I Am state, when there is a sense of impersonal presence. But that sense of impersonal presence is what the Zen folks talk about when they say, "In the beginning when you start Zen the rivers and mountains are rivers and mountains. Then as you progress the rivers and mountains are no longer rivers and mountains." This is the stage of, "Oh it's a dream. It's all one. They're not rivers and mountains, they're Consciousness." That sense of unity as an experiential oneness, an impersonal presence, is an intermediate phenomenal state. And then with the final Awakening or dissolution of the sense of personal doership, "The rivers and mountains become rivers and mountains again." The instrument, the body-mind mechanism, continues acting according to its nature...according to its conditioning...according to its genetic background, combined with all of its subsequent conditioning. But there is no sense of personal doership there at all. And so, the experiences associated with that of oneness, of unity—all of those kinds of associated experiences—are just not relevant. There is no place for them to inhere any longer.

The body-mind mechanism is still aware? Still self-aware? Still responds?

If it could not it would be a slab of meat...

Sure.

Laying there, comatose.

So, you have thoughts occur, your mind is not silent. Is that correct to say?

The brain in this body-mind mechanism functions in essentially the same way as in any other body-mind mechanism. You could say that thoughts occur yet the mind is silent.

You don't get involved in the story.

Yes, there is no involvement by a 'me' but it does get very tricky, because there *is* a type of involvement. I mean, if there wasn't some kind of involvement, there wouldn't be any functioning. A certain amount of involvement is necessary for the functioning. And that's why Ramesh used this notion of the working mind and the thinking mind. It was to make the distinction between the involvement of the working mind which operates the mechanism and which is the instrument of doership, and the thinking mind which considers itself an independent doer and becomes involved in horizontal duration. In the sage, the *thinking mind* is absent. Remember that the working-mind and thinking-mind do not exist. It is a concept. But what Ramesh is pointing to is that this involvement in the result of a thought or action, is not there in the sage. Obviously there is sufficient involvement to handle the task at hand and in what is going on. I mean, if you're going to sell your house, you must get a real estate agent. You must get a sign. To do this, you have to be involved enough in the process, and be able to think ahead, and plan. Then, if you sell it you are going to have to move. Then you best have a mover lined up... all of those kinds of things. In order for the mechanism to function, it has to be able to do those things.

♋   ♋   ♋

MORE OF WAYNE'S STORY

Do you do any practice?

Do I now? I'm afraid this is it. It's a nasty job, but somebody has to do it. *(laughter)*

What were you doing before?

Up until early 1996, I was a moderately successful importer/exporter. And one day, in the stroke of a fax, my business of thirteen years evaporated! And it surprised the shit out of me! *(laughter)* But that's what happened. It went away. And I was left with some extra time on my hands, and I was not at all certain what I was going to be doing next. I was in Bombay in July of that year, for Guru Purnima at Ramesh's. I was just sitting there, minding my own business, and Ramesh announced, "Everybody come back tomorrow. Tomorrow Wayne is giving the talk." And I said, "Oh, really?" I don't know, maybe Ramesh just figured I needed a job. *(laughter)*

Were you importing from India?

No, Korea. It wasn't related to any of this.

Why did you go to India at first?

Alright, we have some time so I'll tell you the story. I had virtually no interest in spiritual matters my entire life. I was an alcoholic, and I was a drug-addict from the time I was sixteen till the time I was thirty five, and that was my basic field of endeavor. *(laughter)* And that's not as funny as it sounds. My whole premise in life was that I was the center of the universe, that I was in charge of my life. I believed it was up to me to make things happen in this world, that I needed to establish my goals, my priorities, my wants, my desires, and then set about getting them! And if I wasn't getting what I wanted, I just needed to try harder. Those were the principles I lived by. And it was so incredibly painful to live that way, that the only way I could survive was to drink and use drugs. But it was killing me. I was drinking a fifth of alcohol a day, and doing a gram of cocaine nearly every day. I had been doing that for a number of years, and I was not getting any healthier. I had to drink in the morning to stop the shakes. I had the dry-heaves every morning while brushing my teeth. That was how I was living. And one day, I was lying in bed at the end of a four day binge, and this obsession that I had had for so many years went away. Poof! Gone! Gone! And I felt it go. It was really gone! And I was faced with a bit of an intellectual problem here. (laughter) If, in fact, I was the master of my destiny, what *did* this to me? I didn't do this to me. I knew I didn't do this to me. This *happened* to me. It was clear that it had happened to me. And I set about finding out what power in the universe, if you will, had done this to *me*!!

So, I started reading, and I read the Tao Te Ching and Huang Po and Chuang Tzu. I was reading everything I could get my hands on. I took up T'ai Chi and tried various kinds of meditation. I was doing all kinds of spiritual things. Then, after about a year and a half of that, a friend came and said, "There is a guy coming from India, and he's giving a talk in Hollywood, and they're only charging a buck. Why don't we go? What have we got to lose?" If they'd been charging ten bucks, I probably wouldn't have gone. *(laughter)* But they were only charging a buck, so I went.

Ramesh got up and stood at the lectern, and he gave this incredibly, mind-bogglingly dry talk. *(laughter)* It was horrible. He was talking about Noumenon and phenomenon, and Consciousness in movement and Consciousness at rest, and I had no background in any of this. I didn't know Nisargadatta Maharaj from the Easter bunny. I didn't know any of the biggies. I had never heard of Ramana Maharshi. I didn't know any of this. And I didn't follow a word that Ramesh said. Yet there was something about the guy that pricked my interest...I wasn't sure what.

I went off on a business trip and when I came back two weeks later, he was giving talks up in Hollywood at Henry Dennison's house. I went up there, and I sat down in front of him. There were only a few other people in the room, and when he started talking I was just absolutely bowled over! In that context, in the intimate confines of that living room, I saw a window into the Infinite. There was a resonance there that was unmistakable. I fell in love! No one was more surprised than I that this had happened. I had fallen in love with a retired banker *(laughter)* from India, who is fortunately a lot less dry in intimate settings than he is when he's lecturing. I mean, it was a whole different atmosphere. And I was hooked. I went back to see him every day. He was there for three months. And I was there twice a day. I was making every possible excuse to be in his presence. I was scheming to be the one to bring him his lunch. I was scheming to get to the house early to ask him some lame question, just so I could be with him. It was really pitiful. *(laughter)*

And there was one guy there, who in Ramesh's presence, had gotten the Understanding. This guy was very close to Ramesh, and he was taking him out for drives and meals. And I hated this guy. No lover has ever been more jealous. I would have killed this guy. *(laughter)*

When Ramesh left Los Angeles, a small group of us were at the airport seeing him off. We were sitting around in the cafe, and the talk turned to all the tapes that had been made over the three months, and it was suggested that a book should be made. "We're going to make a book, and we're going to do this, and transcribe, and print, and publish, and it's going to be great." I'm listening to this, and I'm a businessman, so I say, "You know, you're talking about starting a business here. You've got inventory, you've got cash-flow, you've got order processing." And Henry says, "Wayne, have you ever been in the publishing business?" I said, "No." And Ramesh turns to me and he says, "Not yet." *(laughter)*

Okay. Just to finish your story, your personal story, if I may. For your body-mind mechanism, after some time with Ramesh, the penny dropped, didn't it?

The penny dropped!

And then, um, what would that be like?

It's a good question. The question was, "When the penny DROPPED for me, when I grabbed the brass ring, when I got the WHOLE THING, when I MADE IT to what you ALL WANT, what was it like?" (loud *laughter*) Because that's really the question, isn't it? What am I going to GET, when I get this thing? What's it going to be like? If I have to put up with all this crap, what am I going to get at the end of it? And the fact is, that NOTHING HAPPENS. In my case, there were a variety of experiences when the sense of personal doership fell away but the ultimate Understanding was that *nothing happened* !

There was a tremendous feeling of relief at that moment, an experiential feeling that something had just *changed*. When the identification shifts to the Total, there is no *movement*, there is no subject-object relationship function that will give an experience. The only subject-object experience is through the body-mind mechanism, and what I'm saying is, that the body-mind mechanism does not get enlightened.

After the 'penny drops' the body-mind mechanism experiences phenomenality directly, according to its nature, according to the conditioning both genetic and psychological and environmental. And thus, it reacts according to its nature just as it did before. What is absent is any sense of personal doership.

ᏬᎾ   ᏬᎾ   ᏬᎾ

IS THERE ANY PATTERN TO ENLIGHTENMENT?

One person whom I've heard is enlightened said that he went through a period where he just kind of kicked back and enjoyed life, which was followed by a time of feeling a lot of fear. I remember you saying sometime back that you also went through a certain amount of what seemed to be emotional turmoil just prior to this impersonal event of Awakening. Did you experience any fear? Can you talk about that?

Well, I prefer not to emphasize the 'event' because it's not pertinent to anything...It's a story, just as the person you mentioned told his story, but there is nothing instructive about the story.

I'm just wondering if there's a pattern.

That is why I said that there is nothing instructive about the story. You're not going to determine a cause-effect relationship between these various events. The event of Awakening is an impersonal event. It happens through a body-mind mechanism, and it can happen in all kinds of ways, and there are probably as many stories as there are body-mind mechanisms through which it has happened. But the impulse is always to focus on the experience, in the secret hope that, "Okay, if we can identify what it was that caused the Awakening, then by diligently applying ourselves to duplicating this feat, we can get what we want!"

It's not that...

It is that, precisely!

I was just wondering if your experiencing that emotional turmoil could have been a precursor...

And what I'm telling you is that it is not causative.

It's not? It's different in each case?

Yes.

Okay.

So, if this Enlightenment is a matter of Grace, then why should we seek? Why should we not just give up?

Try giving up! (laughter) *You* didn't ask to become a seeker. The seeking started. So *you* can't give it up. You didn't start it, so you can't give it up! It's the same as having sex with a six hundred pound gorilla...you're not done until the gorilla is done. (laughter)

IS IT A GRADUAL PROCESS?

Does one get closer to realization a little bit at a time?

Well, again, to use one of Ramesh's images: you are climbing a staircase of a hundred and thirty stairs. You take one step at a time. You move up the staircase one step at a time. The movement from the hundred and twenty ninth step to the hundred and thirtieth step is always sudden. If the top one is the hundred and thirtieth one, the arrival at that point is always sudden. Because you've taken that step and now you're there, there's a sudden movement. The fact that you may have started at step one hundred and twenty six, or you may have started at step six, is an accident of birth. But if you were to take that hundred and thirtieth step, it is always sudden. And you never know whether you're on the hundred and twenty second step, or the sixth step, or the hundred and twenty ninth step, until you take the step from the hundred and twenty ninth to the thirtieth.

So you view it as a process of steps?

No, I wouldn't try and put too much weight on this particular image. If you find an image and it hits you as being useful in the moment, then that's great. None of these images are going to bear up under very close scrutiny. They are, as Ramana Maharshi called them, "Thorns used to remove other thorns." You have a thorn embedded in your foot—some concept which is blocking you from understanding—now another concept may be employed by the sage to remove the first concept. And in the deft hands of a sage it may be useful. It may do the desired trick. But in the hands of the unskilled, who take this concept and dig around in there forever, it may create a bloody mess. (laughter) The longer you dig the duller the thorn gets. It is only useful for a deft pick. That's why with any of these concepts, if they don't *(slap)* hit you, if they're not useful in the moment, then let them go. Because to attempt to analyze, and attempt to utilize this idea for your own understanding is not going to get you anywhere.

When people leave Ramesh they frequently say, "Okay Ramesh, I've been here for a week, it has been wonderful, but I must go. Before I go, is there one thing that you can tell me that I can take home with me?" And he would say, "My one piece of advice would be to forget everything you've heard here." Ramesh knows that all of these concepts are just more weight in the backpack.

♋   ♋   ♋

BLISS

When this disidentification happens, what happens?

Well, the body-mind mechanism will continue to respond...

...Respond, but not react.

It does not react in a conscious way. That is true. There's no longer anyone there with a sense that they are reacting. But there is reaction.

So, the latent tendencies might continue to function, albeit they may not be healthy...

Yes, whatever is meant by *healthy*.

...but through a period of time maybe, they become more humorous, or more matter-of-fact.

Perhaps.

So, the bad characteristics aren't going to go away. They are going to continue because that body-mind is made up of that, and it may continue to do that.

That is absolutely correct. They may continue. And what one person calls a bad characteristic, another might consider quite desirable.

With no personal doer, why would that have to be? Why couldn't Consciousness transform them, just by Consciousness itself?

Oh, it could. A body-mind mechanism can be transformed in a variety of ways. It doesn't necessarily require Understanding to happen. You see transformations happening within people all the time.

But the transformation can definitely occur within a no-mind state, or a freedom can't it? The so-called personality, or body-mind traits don't have to stay the same way?

Yes, but there's no one there to be concerned with the body-mind traits one way or the other. That is the salient point.

But don't you still respond to sensation, or...

The body-mind mechanism continues to respond essentially like it always has.

But you're not liking it or disliking it? Because there's nothing there to like or dislike?

Clearly there are preferences on the part of the body-mind mechanism, according to its nature. It may like tomatoes. It may hate liver. It will continue to hate liver and like tomatoes, most likely, after there is Understanding, because it is a quality of the body-mind mechanism. It has a preference for tomatoes over liver.

Krishnamurti answered this by saying the relationship to the way you like your tomatoes changes, but not your like of tomatoes.

Clever man. *(laughter)*

What's the big deal about that? (laughter)

Yeah! What's the big deal about that! *(laughter)*

Yes, so what?

You say, "So what!" That's acceptance. You're accepting that you're not always accepting. In that acceptance, there is peace.

I forget sometimes.

Then there is no acceptance, and you suffer.

I keep getting caught up.

Yes. But at any moment acceptance *can* come and cut off the involvement, then you are in the present! And in the present moment there is only peace.

The big deal is you are at peace all the time?

There is peace here...I get pissed off from time to time. *(laughter)* And still there is peace here all the time.

What about suffering?

There is no suffering.

In this peace do you feel a bliss?

The problem with the word bliss...*(laughter)* ...bliss is synonymous with orgasm, in terms of its general acceptance. The way people think of bliss is this *ahhhh-haaaa* kind of thing. It is not that state. It is not a conditional state. That state—the state that is normally thought of as bliss—is the conditioned opposite of suffering. It is the other side of that same coin. In the Peace that surpasses all understanding, in that Peace, there is no conditioned opposite.

So, then what is the feeling of bliss?

That is a phenomenal sensation. It is the opposite of suffering.

So that's what people call...

That's what most people think of when they think of bliss.

So, when True Enlightenment happens there will be no feeling?

There is a peace that is not conditional; that is not the opposite of suffering.

So, you don't feel anything?

There is no *you* to be concerned. *You* have literally merged with the infinite.

But then when you come back...?

You never come back...because you never went anywhere!

ॐ   ॐ   ॐ

AFTER ENLIGHTENMENT ARE THERE FURTHER DEVELOPMENTS?

Since the Understanding happened, has there been some broadening of the Understanding? Some deepening of the Understanding? Does it arise and fall? Is that just the first step, or have there been any other steps since then?

When the veil drops,

...it drops...

It drops.

Yes, but I always had the understanding that that was just the first step, and then the journey starts.

When there is the Understanding of your True Nature, there is the Understanding of your True Nature. What may happen phenomenally is of no consequence. When you have a dream at night, and in that dream, there is someone who is being tortured, horribly tortured, and you wake up from the dream, are you any longer concerned about what happened to that person who was being tortured? Of course not! That person never existed. You know that person never existed. Why would you have concern for the fate of that person who never existed, or for what happened to him? Nothing *could* happen to him.

No, I'm not talking about that person who was there before the veil dropped.

And what I'm saying is, when the veil drops, there is no one there to be concerned with anything.

So, the process of questioning, does that still occur for you?

No.

...just right now...no more questions?

No more questions.

The reason there are no questions is there is no one to ask them?

If you like, yes.

So you're not saying it's a state of all-knowingness, it's just a state of "Who cares?" No one to care...so there are no questions if there is no one to hear the answers? And yet there seems to be great caring. Maybe there's no one there for any deepening to happen to, but from what I see there is tremendous caring.

There can be. The caring does happen sometimes through this body-mind mechanism.

I imagine there are some that just say, "Well, I'm outta here!"

Oh, yes.

♋   ♋   ♋

LOVE

So what about love?

What about it?

What is that?

(laughter) ...Well...it's on page 35 of *No Way*...

Most of what
You call love
Is just business.

You demand
Sufficient return
On your investment
Or you go elsewhere.

No-one likes to
Suffer a loss.
After all,
If you don't manage
Your portfolio
Who will? *(laughter)*

It's not the sort of thing
You want to leave to chance. *(laughter)*

Problem is
You're always in fear
You're always hedging.

Ram Tzu knows this...

It's a losing proposition
Trying to keep that
Which you haven't got.

What about unconditional Love?

Unconditional Love can only exist in *your* absence. As long as *you* are there, there will be conditions. The only truly unconditional Love, is that of the Guru, because there is no one there to give it.

So is there Love there?

There is Love here. *(silence)* What could be a greater Love than total acceptance?

Now, do you have only a loving experience with everyone, no matter what they are, who they are?

Yes, except the assholes! *(laughter)* Everybody else I like.

You don't like assholes? (laughter)

Absolutely! That's what makes them assholes, when I don't like them! *(laughter)* And still there is total acceptance and unconditional love here.

♋   ♋   ♋

USELESSNESS OF ENLIGHTENMENT

What kind of life does that entity lead if he is not subject to all of the things that I and all of my friends are every day?

But the whole question of the 'entity' leading that life is gone. You think in terms of an entity leading a life.

Yeah...

But there's no entity *there*, either in the sage *or* in the ordinary person. There's only the *appearance* of an entity in the *ordinary person*.

Does the sage experience the same thing that we do?

We have to define what you mean by *the sage*. Are you talking about the body-mind mechanism through which this understanding has happened?

Yes.

Okay. There obviously *is* an experience of something, so, if there's no entity there to *take delivery* of these experiences, then there is simply pure experience.

I was wondering what that would be like.

For whom?

I guess for me! Because it seems kind of like a way of disappearing.

It *is* a way of disappearing. You could *say* it's a way of disappearing, but that which would register the disappearance is gone. That which would experience the disappearance is gone.

If you ask the average person whether they'd like to disappear or not, they would probably become upset.

Yes.

But it seems obvious that this disappearing should be considered something desirable.

Well, I don't know. I wouldn't say so. I would echo Ramesh's sentiment that if you have the choice between getting Enlightenment and getting a million dollars, take the million dollars. Because if you have a million dollars, there will be *somebody* there to enjoy it. But if Enlightenment comes, there's no *one* there to enjoy the Enlightenment.

There's one funny story. About three or four years ago, Ramesh and I were at the racetrack in Bombay commiserating over the fact that I had lost a fairly substantial sum in the stock market. In a typically brilliant assessment of how the market was going to go, I short-sold my shares during the biggest bull market in history, saying, "This will never last." So, I was expressing to Ramesh that I just couldn't pick a stock to save my life, and he was saying that he had had similar experiences. Despite being a very successful banker, his own stocks had never proved to be very lucrative, and our experience that day at the racetrack was no exception. I said, "Ramesh, what good is this Understanding if you can't pick a goddamn horse or a goddamn stock?" And he laughed and said, "Why, it's of no use whatsoever, my boy—no use whatsoever." *(laughter)*

DETACHMENT
AND THE SAGE.

I wonder how is it for you. Are you sometimes identified with the wave? Or is it always that there is a consciousness that sees that you are the ocean? Is there sometimes an identification there? Can you say something about this?

Yes. You think in terms of an enlightened individual. The question is addressed to an enlightened individual, asking, how does this individual, having achieved Enlightenment, respond to life? And what I am saying (and this is not an original thought) is that there is no such thing as an enlightened individual. In the moment of Understanding, the locus of perceived doership drops away from the individual and exposes the Infinite. The body-mind mechanism continues on, much as it always has, responding to the stimulus of life within the manifestation much in the same way that it always has. It is a conditioned apparatus. It was born with certain characteristics which are subsequently altered somewhat through its experiences. It responds to what is happening around it according to its nature, according to its programming. There is no question, when there is Understanding, of any one doing anything. The responses happen through the body-mind mechanism according to the way it is designed to respond.

It would seem to me that this response means that the mind is active.

Okay.

Is that a reality?

There is a mind as part of the body-mind mechanism. There is mental activity within the body-mind mechanism.

And that doesn't alter with the Understanding?

The Understanding is impersonal. The Understanding is transcendent of the thought process of the individual organism.

So if I have Understanding...

You do not have Understanding! *(laughter)*

But if there is Understanding, and I get angry, would my response be to get angry at a specific situation, or something? Is there an acting out of that anger?

If there is anger, it may well be acted out. But the 'I' you are referring to wouldn't be there to believe it was doing it.

*Well, earlier you said that you have..."There is Un-
derstanding here, and I get pissed off."*

There is not Understanding here *(pointing to his
body)* there is Understanding Here. *(pointing to space between him and the listeners)* The Understanding is not
located in the body. It is not fixed in the body. The Understanding is transcendent. That is what I keep
hammering at. The misapprehension is that there is an
enlightened person. *(whispers)* There's no enlightened
person. The 'pissed offedness' is a response of the body-
mind mechanism.

So, there's no personality alteration?

There may be. As with any event in phenomenali-
ty, there may be a shift in the personality. There are shifts
in personality all the time within body-mind mechanisms. Happens all the time. It has nothing whatsoever
to do with Understanding.

*Are you saying there is no enlightened person, yet
there is an enlightened being?*

Well, you're splitting semantic hairs. I am pointing
away from the personalization of Enlightenment as something that can be had by an individual. As long as there
is an individual wanting Understanding, there can be
no Understanding.

*So, if the individuality is gone then there is Enlight-
enment in this person, yet...*

Well, that's where it gets tricky, because after there
is Understanding there is still a personality. If someone
calls Ramesh by name, he turns around, because there is
a personality there. There is identity there to the extent
that that body-mind mechanism is named Ramesh. There
is no sense whatsoever there that Ramesh is the doer of

any of the actions that happen through Ramesh, or that happen through any other body-mind mechanism. There is the Understanding that all there is, is Consciousness.

At a higher level of awareness of how Consciousness is doing things, is there less emotion? It would seem to me that the emotional responses to what happens would start to wear off.

Emotional response is a function or characteristic of the body-mind mechanism. Some body-mind mechanisms are emotional by nature, and they react very strongly to whatever happens within their view. Others are practically impervious to what they see, unmoved by virtually anything. And I would say that in general, the sage is *more* involved in What Is in the moment, because there is no filter there of, "Oh, this is just the functioning of Totality. It's all just illusion." There's no intellectualization involved in the sage's present moment. Every aspect of the dream is real within the context of the dream. It is immediate, it is now, and it is an expression of the one Consciousness. So, the sage doesn't make that kind of distinction that, "Oh, the Supreme Reality is God or Consciousness, and this world is a pale, worthless vale of tears that will simply pass and is hardly worth noticing, because what's truly important is God." The sage sees that all there is, literally, is *this*, because God has no existence or quality in any separate way, in any measurable way. This world is God made manifest.

There's basically just a reaction on the part of the sage to whatever is going on?

Yes, a very pure, immediate action. There is *pure doership*. That's why earlier when someone was asking me, "What were you doing when you were silently looking around?" the precise answer is that I was doing nothing.

Yet, there *was* whatever was happening without any sense of, "*I* am doing that," or, "I shouldn't have done that," or, "I should have done that better." *(laughter)*

It seems that one who had the Understanding would also lose his guilt over things, because he would stop holding things to himself.

Yes, both guilt and pride go. So you can say that there is true humility. True humility is knowing that "I am not the doer."

When the Understanding occurs, it seems to me that the body-mind mechanism that's left, would be left with a sort of an impersonal outlook. It would lose concern for the day-to-day bullshit.

Who would be not left with an interest? That is the crux of the question. Who is it that you think has this Enlightenment?

Intellectually I understand that, but I guess the point I'm trying to make is that the body-mind mechanism that is left would certainly have a profound shift in outlook over the day-to-day world. It would seem that there would have to be some effect on the way we look at things. I mean, how could you take anything seriously any longer?

If the body-mind mechanism has a serious aspect to it, has certain values to it, it will respond according to those qualities. There is no choice being made by either the body-mind mechanism of a *jnani* or by the body-mind mechanism in which there is a sense of personal doership. There is only the *illusion* of choice within the body-mind mechanism of one who has not awakened. Your question presumes that the *jnani* will *choose* to act differently with his newfound knowledge. But he is not choosing anything.

Is it possible that the sage's body-mind mechanism is on the pendulum shaft somewhere instead of at the fulcrum?

We're sort of mixing metaphors there, because what rides on the pendulum shaft is the sense of personal doership. The body-mind mechanism, of course, operates in phenomenality and is part of all of the movement. Actually, I hadn't really thought about it in this context before, but I suppose you could say that the body-mind mechanism's movement *is* the movement of the pendulum—that it *is* this functioning in phenomenality. What is absent in the sage is any sense of personal doership. It's just not there. There is nothing to move either up into the experience of impersonal awareness or back down into the experience of involvement. It is gone, period.

♋   ♋   ♋

DESIRE AND EMOTION

Wayne, after Enlightenment does wanting arise any more?

Wanting arises as a function of the organism. The organism is programmed and conditioned in such a way as to have desires and some of them are associated with the body such as the need for food or drink or sex or warmth. Those kinds of desires are aspects of the body built into the mechanism.

Depending on the nature of the mechanism, those are survival ones. Do the wants exceed that as well?

You mean like a want for an 'In 'n Out' burger specifically, or the want for sushi, which are somewhat down the scale of survival. *(laughter)* Those are specific kinds of wants. There *are* specific kinds of desires that arise.

So wanting an 'In 'n Out' burger and not being able to have an 'In 'n Out' burger...

...may cause frustration in the body-mind mechanism. When a desire or want is not met, frustration may result. All of these things happen as a functioning of the mechanism. Now, the question is whether there is a sense of doership associated with any of that. Is there any sense of it being *my* desire for an 'In 'n Out' burger, or is there simply a desire for an 'In 'n Out' burger ?

But the involvement, how long the frustration lasts, that's the thinking mind becoming involved. Does that get cut off?

Well, it doesn't get cut off, it is not even there. The involvement is the thought, "What is going to become of me if I don't get an 'In 'n Out' burger? *(laughter)* Will I be able to survive? Will I be able to handle the frustration associated with not getting an 'In 'n Out' burger? Will I freak out? Will it turn me into some kind of desperate crazed kind of creature I don't want to be?" All of that involvement just doesn't happen.

Does the irritation continue for say 5 minutes? Later are you thinking "Damn if I could only have had that 'In 'n Out' burger?" Does the irritation arise again?

It may arise again. Sure. The whole question has to do with what is the response of the enlightened being to a frustration or to a desire or to a want. I would say what we need to focus on is that there aren't any enlightened beings. The effect of this falling away of personal doership on the body-mind mechanism is quite varied, and so it is difficult to determine what the response of a particular body-mind mechanism will be. You are asking, "How will this mechanism behave? How will it respond? How will it react?" What I am saying is that it will react according to its nature. What is absent in the body-mind mechanism *where Enlightenment has happened* is the sense of doership, the sense that I am involved in any of this stuff. The response is happening as part of the nature of the body-mind mechanism. You could say there is a recognition of desire, but even to say there is a recognition that there is a desire for an 'In 'n Out' burger is to go too far. *That* which would recognize that desire is happening is gone. There just *is* the desire for an 'In 'n Out' burger. There is the attendant frustration of not getting an 'In 'n Out' burger when one is desired but not available but that is experienced as just a part of What Is! And you say, "I want to be enlightened because I don't like the frustration, the frustration frustrates me and makes me unhappy! I don't like being frustrated, I don't like being unhappy, I don't like that feeling of not getting what I want!" and so, "If I'm enlightened, then I'm not going to have to experience that any more," which is both true and not true. It is true to the extent that you are not going to have to experience that any more but the relief or satisfaction that you would get from not experiencing it, is not there either! *(laughter)*

Even when there is no involvement, enlightened sages cry too, don't they?

Absolutely. There is a great Milarepa story about one of Milarepa's disciples who is walking across a field, and he sees Milarepa sitting in the middle of the field crying inconsolably. He rushes up and says, "Master,

Master what could possibly be the matter?" Milarepa looks up and says, "I've just gotten news that my son is dead." The disciple sits for a moment and then says, "But Master you've been telling us that this is all just a dream, all just an illusion." Milarepa replies, "Yes it *is* a dream, it *is* an illusion, but the death of one's son is the most painful illusion of them all."

It seems like I can have some understanding of what is really happening but there is still something that is here reacting to all of this stuff, so I can't really totally blow it all off.

Right. The body-mind mechanism reacts according to its nature. Most human beings, when losing that which they love, experience loss and pain. You can say the sage operates through the human body, and, therefore, is subject to all the same emotional kinds of experience as any other body-mind mechanism.

That is why I like this Advaita teaching because in the past there have always been these ideas that Enlightenment means being way above anything having to do with any human form.

Yes, well that seems to be a very common notion. People take their leaders, be they spiritual or religious or whatever and put them up on a pedestal. Then they take secret delight in seeing them fall. And fall they will. The position on the pedestal is unsustainable...unless, the one on the pedestal is dead.

What I really appreciated about my experience with Ramesh was to be able to spend the amount of time that I did with him, not only in the talks but also over the course of the day. I was able to experience the sage as a body-mind mechanism through which this teaching comes. There was still tremendous love for the Guru but there was also a much broader based love, one that accepted the human characteristics of the body-mind mechanism too. So, there were no unrealistic notions of omniscience or omnipotence or moral purity according to some arbitrary standard. There was a body-mind mechanism with characteristics and qualities, a nature that was clearly a product of its upbringing, as well as a combination of its basic inherent nature. Now, Ramesh's inherent nature happens to be quite gentle, at least a surface gentleness and courtliness. Underneath there is a core of strength. But there is quite a soft wrapping, he will take a lot before snapping, becoming angry.

It seems that a lot of Teachers are pretty egocentric.

Some are. You have a picture of what a sage is supposed to be like. He is supposed to react this way and not react that way. He may or may not be sexually inclined, or he may or may not be interested in other quote 'mundane' aspects of the world such as money or property. Lack of interest is supposed to be a mark of enlightenment but there are a lot of body-mind mechanisms that are not interested in any of those things who are not sages.

The body-mind mechanism of a sage responds according to its characteristics. The characteristics of the body-mind mechanism of a sage before and after Understanding, are likely to be essentially the same.

It seems that sages don't see things as either right or wrong. They see it all as part of the whole. I think that's what our job is here, just to play our part, and to be what we are.

How could we be anything different! *(laughter)* It's an easy job.

Can you talk just a little bit about emotional rela-
tionships after Enlightenment? Are emotions by this
body-mind mechanism sort of placed in oneness?

Yes. You see, when I talk about Enlightenment, the
Enlightenment I talk about here is not the personal enlightenment that is the experiential feeling of oneness in
which you feel "I am one with everything." It is outside
of that paradigm. The Understanding incorporates the
fact that all of these body-mind mechanisms are created
by Consciousness and operated by Consciousness, and
that every thought, every action, every emotion, and
every response is the thought, the action, the emotion,
and the response of Consciousness. What separates the
body-mind mechanism of the sage from the ordinary
person is that, in the sage, there is no sense of personal
doership attributed to any of the thoughts, or actions, or
emotions. These are a response by the mechanism, and
the mechanism responds according to its nature—which
is its genetic makeup combined with its subsequent conditioning. And the subsequent conditioning is dynamic,
so that in this exact instant, this body-mind mechanism
will react according to the sum total of its genetics and
all its conditioning up to this moment. A moment from
now, however, another thought will have gone through
the mind or another hormonal change will have taken
place in the body, so the organism will be different, and
will thus react to the same stimulus differently. Whereas
in the previous instant it may have been very passive, in
the next instant it may react with anger over the same
exact impulse, the same exact input. The reaction is utterly and completely different. Now, mind you, the
mechanistic nature of all of this is not *seen* as such by the
sage, because the sage is not in any way separate from
it. The sage is simply an instrument of it, without any
overlay of doership. That is the only difference.

That means that the sage does not identify with the thoughts that go by, or the emotions?

You can say that. The body-mind mechanism identifies with the thoughts and the emotions, they're part of the whole package. They're being experienced as part of the package. But that experience is part of the overall functioning of Totality, which is where the identification of the sage lies.

It occurs to me that maybe the sage is the only person who really enjoys life.

Well, Ramesh says that in one of the Hindu Scriptures the sage is described as the *Mahabhogi*—the supreme enjoyer—for the very reason that there is no filter. Yet it could also be said that he is the supreme sufferer.

But if he's not identifying with anything, then how could he suffer?

You're right. A more precise phrase would be the supreme experiencer of pain, because there is no involvement in the sage. The sage is the supreme experiencer of pleasure and pain, simply because there is no filter involved between the experience and the experiencer. You could say that the suffering is a secondary experience. It comes about as a reaction to the immediate experience. When you experience pain and then there is involvement, the involvement says, "This pain is intolerable. I'm not going to be able to stand this. What happens if this goes on for weeks? I'll go nuts!" That is suffering, and that is what the sage does not do. There is no mechanism in the sage for that to happen.

I would imagine regrets and certain fears disappear completely?

Yes.

How did it affect your relationships with people once the struggle had finished, had dropped away? Was there any major change in the way you related to people?

My wife is nodding her head. I can't tell! I mean, from a personal standpoint, I don't *register* those changes. I suppose I wasn't, and remain not particularly interested. Whatever personality characteristics changed were more noticeable by others than by me. But personally—I think I turned into a hell of a great guy. *(laughter)*

Where's your wife? I want her to tell...

You might hear a different story from her. *(laughter)* But I'm sure as the seeking eased, I became more relaxed. I'm sure that translated into my relationships with others. The important thing to understand about the changes that come about, is that changes come about in every body-mind mechanism throughout their lives. Events happen, and the responses by the various organisms are quite different. You can't say that when the seeking falls away, *this* list of personality characteristics ensues or that when the Awakening happens, then the personality becomes *this way.* Look, you have Ramana Maharshi—totally kicked back, you know. He's in Southern India, laying back on his tiger skin, answering a few questions, swatting a few flies with his...oh, *brushing* them. Not swatting. I mean, he was a saint, after all! *(laughter)*

Oh, he didn't do it. Somebody else did it for him.

Somebody else did it. Even better. He didn't even have to do his own fly work! He's totally kicked back, he has someone else shooing his flies away, and he answers a few questions. He asks people who it is who's asking the question, and—life is peaceful! A very gentle, easy kind of personality. Now you have Nisargadatta Maharaj. And Maharaj is a very *different* kind of personality. He has a very aggressive nature. And when you come to him and you ask that same question for the fourth time in a row, he will yell at you to get OUT OF HIS SAT-SANG! *(laughter)* Because that's the nature of the mechanism. And the basic fundamental nature of the mechanism is not necessarily changed by the falling away of the sense of personal doership, because it is not the body—it is not the body-mind mechanism that is enlightened!

I can say it over and over and over and over again, and it cannot be said too often. When you think about this Awakening, which is an impersonal event which happens through a body-mind mechanism you *have* to assume, because of your own lifetime experience, that there is someone there for whom this experience happens. You can't imagine an impersonal happening of that kind, or what an impersonal experiential state would be, because there is no such thing as an impersonal experiential state. It is incomprehensible, literally incomprehensible. Yet, that is what it is and after Enlightenment, the body-mind continues to function according to its nature in the moment.

Like your finger print doesn't change ?

Your finger print doesn't change but your *personality* is in constant flux.

℠   ℠   ℠

MEMORY AND THE SAGE

What about memory? Do you remember yesterday's stuff?

No, but I didn't remember yesterday's stuff before this Understanding either! *(laughter)*

Do you remember this morning's stuff?

Yes, of course. Some of it. There *is* a mind here... feeble though it may be.

But normally you don't worry about it, or think about it?

Thoughts come. They may be thoughts that have their origin in yesterday, they may be thoughts that have their origin in a week ago, they may be thoughts that have their origin in somebody's previous life. They're just thoughts in the brain! And then they're reacted upon according to this particular body-mind mechanism's characteristics.

I'm just wondering how much of a sense of memory for events is there post Enlightenment.

Memory is a function of the mind. In the sage there is still a mind.

Yes.

If there is no mind left in the sage, the sage can't function. If the sage can't remember, if the sage doesn't have memory, he doesn't know his name. He doesn't know who his wife is. He doesn't know where he lives. He doesn't know that this is his begging bowl and that this is his cell phone. He doesn't have any ability to make distinctions between things, because that information resides in memory, in mind. And the sage still has a mind. All the sage lacks is a sense of personal doership. The sense that *I am the doer*. There is only pure doership, through the body-mind mechanism of the sage.

♋   ♋   ♋

ACCEPTANCE

Is there just more acceptance?

Yes, there *is* acceptance, but not acceptance at the level of the doer. You see, the doer accepts—when there is acceptance in an identified individual that acceptance cuts off involvement by the *me*, and brings one *present*. For the body-mind mechanism in which there is no sense of personal doership, there is *never* any involvement by the *me*, therefore, acceptance can be said to be always there.

Do you ever get tense about anything? (silence) You have to think that long...? (laughs)

I was riding with my sixteen-year-old, who was driving on the freeway for the first time, and I was grabbing onto the door handle. *(laughs)* So yes, I get tense.

But most of the things that happen to you, are they pretty impersonal?

No! They're intensely personal. Intensely personal.

Really? But you don't take them personally?

No. I don't.

That's the key.

That is simply what happens. There is no involvement, because that which carries forward into involvement is absent. There is, whatever is there. So, there is the experience and then it gets cut off. It doesn't get pursued into horizontal involvement.

So, if you want to ask what is the difference, well that is the difference. But the fact is that this body-mind mechanism reacts according to its nature. It has a temperament, it has characteristics that are the product of its genetic background and all of the experiences that it has had up to this precise instant. And so it will respond, in this instant, according to all of that combined.

Then this instant gets added to that, and in the next instant it may react completely differently because of what happened in this instant, that changed the temperament of the mechanism, changed the responsive nature of the mechanism, so that in the next instant it will respond to the same stimulus entirely differently. And that is the way it is with everyone. That is how these body-mind mechanisms work. A slight hormonal change, a new thought, another input of some kind...you see something, it registers and it changes who you are. Utterly. After that your response to things, your reactions are totally changed.

But you're not identified with what your body-mind does...

There is no identification as the doer. There is just pure action. Through every body-mind mechanism there is only pure action. The only difference is whether there is a sense that is *my* action, that *I* am doing it, or not. That is why it's so hard to pick a sage out of a line up. *(laughs)*

I'm not sure I agree with that.

Okay. You don't need to agree. I have no desire to convince you of anything.

So you're not hooked? You're never hooked into any-thing? Is that true?

It depends who you're asking the question of, you see. The body-mind mechanism gets hooked into all kinds of things because of its nature. It's a reactive mechanism. So, it responds. By *hooking*, do you mean, does anything affect the sage?

Yes.

Of course! The body-mind mechanism of the sage is not a lump of human tofu! It's not a bland, colorless blob with no inherent qualities of its own.

You're not a tofu lover?

Tofu strikes me as a very difficult thing to LOVE. *(laughter)*

But you never lose contact with the fact that you're not the body-mind mechanism?

Once again, who is this *you* that you are talking to?

Well, who's talking?

You see, if you think in terms of the body-mind mechanism of the sage as being enlightened, you've missed the point. There are no enlightened body-mind mechanisms. There are just body-mind mechanisms. En-lightenment is an impersonal event that happens through a particular body-mind mechanism. And what the ef-fect on that body-mind mechanism might be is quite variable. So it is more precise to say that the Understand-ing is Here *(pointing to space between himself and speaker).*

The Understanding is Here. The Understanding isn't here *(pointing to his body)*.

Lost me.

Good. You see the Understanding is Here. Right Here *(points to space between himself and the group)*

You mean here, big here? Or right here?

HERE! (laughs)

♋   ♋   ♋

PERCEPTION

There was something I was thinking about the other day. I have a particular type of perception now, but after Enlightenment happens, everything is known to be the same, made of the same stuff. What does that stuff look like if it's all the same stuff? I realize that I can't have the complete understanding intellectually with the mind, but is there something close that can explain it?

The sensory perception is essentially the same. What I'm picking up in my visual field coming through my eyes and registering on the retinas and being transferred by the optic nerve to whatever portion of the brain registers those things and makes some kind of sense out of the image, I am assuming is a fairly universal process amongst human beings. Human beings have similar physiology, but not precisely the same. For example, I'm red/green color-confused. The term 'color-blind' is politically incorrect. I confuse certain colors because whatever sensory receivers are in the eye are not there in sufficient number to register a difference that other people's eyes can distinguish. Therefore, the perception is obviously different in my body than it is in your body if you're not red/green color-confused. Now, because that color-confusion tends not to have tremendous impact, we go about our daily lives with the appearance of having similar perceptions of things, even though there may be a wide difference in the way you and I would see the same scene. So, from that level, none of us see things in precisely the same way. To a certain degree, our physiology will affect how we perceive something, and our preferences, knowledge and interests will also affect how we see or what will catch our attention.

For instance, before I built this house, I did not have any real architectural appreciation. I would drive down the street, and I wouldn't see any architectural qualities to the buildings. They were just structures. Occasionally one might stand out if it was painted a certain way or was particularly dramatic. The way I perceived things as I walked down the street three years ago versus the way I perceive them today when I walk down the same street, is entirely different. This is as a result of a change in conditioning of the organism. Having learned about roof lines and window options and facade materials, I see things differently now. A change in the conditioning changes the perception, changes the awareness of the environment.

We assume that humans see things similarly, but in fact we see things very differently. Living with someone of the opposite sex can be a good reminder of this. (laughter) The event of Awakening does have an effect in terms of the conditioning of the organism, but what that effect is will vary from organism to organism. It need not have any more significance in regard to the changing of perception than would the building of a house change your architectural perception. The misconception is that when there is this Awakening, *all* is seen as the One, that all is seen to be the same, distinctions disappear.

Everything you see is yourself.

But Enlightenment is a state of Beingness, not a way of seeing things. The state of the body-mind mechanism of the sage is a state that is in duality. It is not a state of Beingness, it is a state of functioning. The body-mind mechanism of the sage is a functional object.

Then the seeing of Truth is not by the functional object?

There is a seeing of Truth that is an experience by a functional object. The Knowing is not by the functional object. The Knowing is a transcendent Knowing that is completely independent of the functional object. That is why there are no enlightened individuals. The seeing of objects (including itself) is by the body-mind mechanism.

Then who is that Enlightenment happening to? I'd have to say it's happening to me, but it's not the me that's conditioned or whatever. Or maybe it is. Can I ask that question?

There is a question in there, but my answering it won't give you anything that you need. What you don't need is more *framework* in which to put What Is. The *aim* of Advaita is the breaking down of that framework, not the creation of a new context for the experience, you see?

♋   ♋   ♋

USING WORDS

I'm having the thought that I want to hear you keep talking, but you talk about Understanding being something other than words.

Yes, it is. Yet the words are part of it too.

It couldn't happen without the words?

Oh, it very well could. But not in this moment it couldn't, because the words are there. *(laughter)*

Can I say something?

Why not?

In a way, as you said before, this is all really bullshit. All the talk is like eating the menu card in the restaurant, instead of enjoying the meal, isn't it? It just satisfies the mind somehow and the intellect or whatever, but it doesn't do the job.

No-o?

No offense, you know, just...

Of course it doesn't do the job! It doesn't get you what you want. Because what you want is not gettable by any means—even eating the meal instead of the menu card. But what we are engaged in here today, is menu card eating. That's what's happening! Menu card eaters have come *(laughter)* and menu card is being served.

So we'll have our last course of menu cards tomorrow. Perhaps you'll dine with me again then.

ॐ   ॐ   ॐ

I Knew We Would Be Friends

As soon as you opened your mouth
And I heard your voice

I knew we would be
Friends.

The first time, dear seeker, I heard
You laugh,

I knew it would not take me long
To turn you back into
God.

Hafiz

The disciples were full of questions about God.

Said the master, "God is Unknown and the Unknowable. Every statement about him, every answer to your questions, is a distortion of the truth."

The disciples were bewildered. "Then why do you speak about God at all?"

"Why does the bird sing?" said the Master.
Anthony de Mello

There would be no such thing as fake gold
if there were no real gold somewhere.
Sufi saying

Sages are not defined by what they SAY
But by what they ARE.
Wayne

You come seeking
You go
Empty handed
For there is
Nothing here.

Only the rare one
Not looking for something
Will share
Ram Tzu's worthless treasure.

SEVEN

Guru and Disciple

HOW WAYNE BEGAN TALKING

How did you begin these meetings? Did someone just start coming, and then someone else started coming, and from that things sort of developed?

Well, what happened was that in 1996, a few months after my business disappeared, I went to India to visit Ramesh. He was speaking on Guru-Purnima, the day that one goes and honors the Guru, and at the end of the talk, he said, "You should all come back tomorrow, tomorrow Wayne's giving the talk."

He graduated *you?*

More like he *outed* me. *(laughter)* He was somewhat fond of doing that anyway. He would say to people, "Oh, have you read that book, *No Way* by Ram Tzu? *There's* Ram Tzu!" So, people would pop up at my house from time to time, but I managed to make it dull enough so they didn't come back.

Anyway, I said to him, "Ramesh, you're doing a masterful job at teaching. As long as you're around, for me to talk about this teaching seems impertinent. And he said, "Nonsense, my dear boy, nonsense! If they come, talk to them." So, I felt that I was pretty safe. *(laughter)* But the next day people came and I talked and I figured that was the end of it. Then a week after I returned to the states, somebody called from Atlanta and said "We've got a small group here and we heard that you are talking. Could you come to Atlanta and talk?" I said, "Well, send me a ticket and I'll come." They sent me a ticket and I went, and the phone has been ringing ever since, with people inviting me here and there.

And you will keep doing this as long as people keep showing up?

Yes, I suppose so. Who knows what will happen? I'm just taking it as it comes. So far, it seems to be what is happening. A few people have been very generous and have made donations so that I don't have to commit my time to a regular job and I can travel and do this. As long as that continues, and people come, I guess I'll continue to do it. I don't know. Right now, this talking is what is happening.

Did you notice prior to that moment when Ramesh asked you to speak that people resonated with you in regard to the teaching or the Understanding?

I rarely talked about it with people.

Well, even if you didn't talk about it?

A few people noticed that there was something going on here, and every once in a while somebody would clearly be resonating.

A few years ago I was on an airplane and the flight attendant was coming down the aisle towards me and our eyes met and held for a bit and she got quite a jolt. The resonance was profound.

A while later after she had finished the meal service she came back and kneeled next to my seat and said, "I don't know what that was all about, but I just want you to know that I am very grateful! Thank you for being here."

It was a very beautiful moment in which the Resonance was experienced outside of a *spiritual* context.

Was there any desire within you to begin teaching?

Not particularly. It wasn't happening because it wasn't time. There was certainly no impulse at all.

None?

None.

It just happens when it happens. I guess you could say that about anything.

Yes, you certainly could.

I haven't met Ramesh. Is he like a lot of men from India that we have met? He looks very pious, very spiritual, like a very holy man.

He is a sweet guy. He's really a lovely man—very patient, very present, but without any trappings. There is no pretense. There is no *holiness* particularly surrounding him, certainly none that he fosters. I felt a profound holiness about him, but it's a holiness that I would feel in a tropical waterfall, something that is very pure and present but without the stereotypical trappings of costumes and incense.

Thank you.

♋   ♋   ♋

ADORATION AND VULNERABILITY

I have these fantasies of what it must be like to be in a room, like you sitting here, with twelve to fifteen people who adore me. Then I think I know what Wayne would say, he would say, "They are not adoring me, adoring is going on. It really has nothing to do with me or you." And I like that because I don't want to be in a position of adoring somebody. It makes one vulnerable.

Sure, that is right. Of course, adoration happening through you makes you vulnerable also. Everything that has a joyous, wondrous, beautiful, ecstatic component to it, also carries with it the opposite potential for you to be hurt, betrayed, wounded, crushed, disappointed. You are very fortunate that I am a hell of a nice guy. *(laughter)*

But you are right. The relationship carries with it the potential for all kinds of 'abuse' whereby people get 'taken advantage of.' That was one of my concerns when I went to see Ramesh in India for the first time. It was my first day in Bombay. I had already spent two and a half months with him in LA, sitting with him in talks like this, coming every day, but this was the first time I was going to see him in India. I was in the Shalimar Hotel having my breakfast. I was to see Ramesh at ten o'clock

and I was sitting there thinking about how the hell someone with my rational mind and cynical nature had found
himself here, in this Bombay hotel room, about to go to
be with a Guru, and how incredible it was that it was *me*
doing that. It just seemed so out of character for me and
with this mental process came the fear, "What if he wants
my stuff?" I had a really cool new red Chrysler convert-
ible, just a few months old. I thought, "What if he wants
my car? What if he asks me to give him my car? Am I
serious about this deal?" I mean, "Am I really surrendering myself or is it, 'Okay, you be my Guru as long as
you do things that clearly benefit me, and if you diverge
from that, if you want my stuff, then I take a hike?'" I
could pay lip service to, "Oh yes, I'm going to surrender
utterly and completely," but the question in my mind
was, "What would I do if he asks me to leave my family
and come here and live here? I have a wife and two kids
and my kids are little. What if he asks me to devote myself to service here and not be with my family? What
would I do? What if he wants to have sex with me? What
would I do?" I mean, these were concerns. I didn't know
how to deal with all this.

This was all before you even walked in?

Yes, this was all mental activity but it was pointing
to a very fundamental concern. Then there was a shift
that happened and I cannot pinpoint where the shift
occurred but there was a surrender that happened. I realized it on the morning I was due to leave Bombay at
the end of that first trip. I was sitting in the same hotel
room about to go see Ramesh to say good-bye and I realized that there was a new desire there. The desire was
simply to be of service, to give, and what was to be given
was not important. In that surrender there was tremendous freedom, one of the most exhilarating and freeing
experiences of my life, when the sense of, "What can I

give him?" replaced that question of, "What might he take from me?"

What happened when you walked in?

It was a total non issue. Obviously, he didn't want anything from me.

Not even sex, huh?

Not even sex, as hard as that is to imagine. *(laughter)*

♋   ♋   ♋

RESONANCE

Why do I feel like I do about you? I can't articulate exactly what I mean.

Well, if you *like* the feeling, then you can call it Grace. *(laughter)*

I really want to be here every time there's a meeting, but I can't right now. Every time there's a satsang, I want to be here, or I want to be wherever you are. But because of the way my life is presently, I can't.

That's what is happening, both the desire and the *unfulfillment* of the desire to attend satsang all the time...

But I don't feel bad about it. I don't feel that I'm missing anything, necessarily.

...and the not feeling bad about it are all part of the functioning of Totality. If there is a strong desire and it's not being fulfilled, there can be a feeling of disappointment or emptiness or deep longing. So, the nature of the mechanism at this particular moment will determine what is experienced.

I've had a few people ask me why I want to come here, and I say, "I don't know, I just like being there." I never felt like this about any other teacher. And you seem so regular to me. I like that. I didn't think it would be like that.

Yes, I know what you mean. Whenever I thought about what a Guru looks like I always pictured somebody like Rajneesh. Now *there's* somebody who *looks* like a Guru—the beard, and the eyes, and the costumes, and all that. You can look at him and say, "Now *there's* a Guru." All the visual cues are there. So, when Ramesh pops up—at least he's *Indian*, that was good!—he was dressed in a blue vest with a white shirt underneath it, and was just a little unassuming guy with no facial hair, no doe-eyed gaze; just a guy who had been a bank president and a husband and father. He was not as I had envisioned an Indian Guru.

I consider myself to be fortunate to have met Ramesh. Regardless of what he looked like, what my preconceptions of him were, and the fact that he wasn't at all consistent with my image of how things ought to be— ultimately it didn't really matter, he was my Guru. I could no more have made it *not* happen than I could have made it happen. It was clear that it was something I hadn't done. If I had designed it, it would have looked very different.

So, you just find the ones that resonate to your way of thinking a sage should be or...?

Well, you say you find him but the Resonance is either there or it is not. Your finding him either happens or it doesn't. The inclination or desire to even look either happens or it doesn't. And there may be a strong desire to look or a very casual one where you are mildly interested and then all of a sudden the teacher appears and there is this Resonance. You don't have to necessarily be a seeker who is running around India from ashram to ashram.

I never found that necessary.

Yes, lots of people haven't found that necessary. And lots of people who have roamed around India going from ashram to ashram have not found their true Guru.

૭   ૭   ૭

RESONANCE CREATES THE GURU

How important is the Guru?

Important for what purpose?

For Awakening, Enlightenment.

Having a relationship with a teacher, of the kind that I've described, one with whom you have Resonance, is incredibly pleasurable. The question of usefulness is related to an objective. Something's usefulness or lack of usefulness is measured in relation to whether it gets you closer to where you want to go. This awakening carries no rules. Ramana Maharshi had a Guru that was a mountain. He had Resonance with that mountain. There was an incredible depth of feeling that he had in relation to the mountain. The Guru arises in the resonance between the seeker and some other object. This object may be a human form or some other form. What is important to remember is that the object we *call* the Guru —is not in fact the Guru. The Guru is that which arises in the Resonance between the two objects. For all the people passing Ramana Maharshi on the street, for whom there was no Resonance, there was no Guru. So, you can say that it is the disciple who creates the Guru, in his relationship with that object which is the other half of that Resonance.

Do you mean the Resonance creates the Guru?

Yes. In the Resonance that exists between the sage and the disciple...in that Resonance the Guru is created. Without the disciple, the sage is just another body-mind mechanism eating and sleeping and doing what body-mind mechanisms do.

Yeah, but nobody is at home.

There never *is* anybody at home, *(laughter)* in *any* of the body-mind mechanisms. What is there in the ordinary person is a hypnotic suggestion, this Divine Hypnosis, which is a sense of personal doership. That sense of personal doership is a belief. It's a false one. There exists no personal doership. There is merely a sense of it. But there *is no* personal doership on the part of any of the body-mind mechanisms. When that which never existed is revealed as not existing, nothing has changed.

So, no disciple, no Guru?

No disciple, no Guru. They are part of a singular movement in Consciousness.

The habit is to accuse you of being the Guru.

Yes.

But that's not the case?

There is the experience for you of my being the Guru, because in *between* this body-mind mechanism and that body-mind mechanism the Guru is made manifest.

It happens in the space between us?

Yes.

It's phenomenal expression is between these body-mind mechanisms?

Yes.

But the Guru is not objective?

That is absolutely correct.

Love is the Guru?

Yes.

Felt.

Yes.

That's quite beautiful.

Isn't it?

Yes. Yes it is. Yes it is.

It was very beautifully put, too.

Thank you.

♋   ♋   ♋

THE NATURE OF RESONANCE

This Resonance, is it a body-mind phenomenon thing, or is it something else?

The Resonance is, in fact, a phenomenal event. It is a phenomenal occurrence which has that mystical quality. I say, 'mystical' because we don't have a better word for it—that ineffable quality that is this connection with That which is the underlying Source and substance of everything. Now, where it gets tricky of course, is that everything is That. There is nothing that is not That. Yet

in this relation, in this connection between some phenomenal objects, be they human or a mountain, where
there is this Resonance, there is an experience of That.
There is a connection with That. There is a seeing of That,
a knowing of That.

*The seeing and the knowing, that's the phenome-
nal thing...*

Yes.

*And if there is this Resonance, if it is real, then
does that phenomenal aspect, the seeing and the knowing fade with time, or is it in some way permanent?*

Any experience, anything in phenomenality fades
with time. Everything does.

*So, the Resonance may not be apparent all of the
time, because the external aspect may fade? Is it the
case then that in the Guru-disciple relationship, if there
is physical separation it may fade?*

It may. That is part of the reason why it is such a
joy to be in the physical presence of the Guru.

*And yet the Resonance, if it is real, is unmistakable
at the time.*

Yes. When it happens, you know it. It's one of those
things that, if you've experienced it then there's really
no need to describe it. If you haven't experienced it, all
the description in the world isn't going to tell you what
it is. Which doesn't necessarily stop us from talking about
it.

*Does the Resonance happen for the sage as well as
the disciple?*

In other words, does the sage experience something in connection with the disciple? And the answer is, yes, there *is* an experience, because in the case of the body-mind mechanism that is the other half of the Guru-disciple relationship, that which we call the sage, there may well be a phenomenal experience of that connectedness, as it is made manifest in the disciple. In other words there may well be a response in the sage to the experience of Resonance reflected by the disciple. And for the sage this is generally a pleasurable response.

♋   ♋   ♋

RESONANCE WITH RAMESH

Now, it is interesting that when I met Ramesh, I had been a seeker for about fifteen months. I had started doing T'ai Chi, sitting in meditation and doing other spiritual things and then a flier came in the mail. I went to see Ramesh, and I fell in love with him. Which is...*ridiculous*. Not only that, I went to see him every day and he was talking thirteen times a week, two talks a day, six-and-a-half days (they gave him Sunday afternoon off). They worked him like a dog the first two-and-a-half months he was in the States. I was there for virtually every session. And after a couple of weeks of being up there every day, listening to him, I found myself writing him this poem:

> Who would have thought
> That I'd fall in love
> With a bespectacled banker
> From Bombay?
> Ridiculous! Ludicrous!
> I must be out of my mind.

I'm married! I'm a father!
An international businessman! A cynic!
Yet here I find myself
Flitting about you
With all the volition
Of a moth at a flame

Wondering...
Afraid...
Secretly hoping...
That this *me* will get too close
And immolate.

That's beautiful.

I took this poem and I folded it up into an itty-bitty little package, and then at the end of the talk I handed it to Ramesh and I ran, because it was without a doubt the lamest thing I had ever done in my entire life! *(laughter)* It was just stupid. And I knew he was going to think that it was ridiculous, but I couldn't help myself. And he later told me that in coming to the States (this was his first visit) he had a real question in his mind whether the kind of relationship that was so common in India— this Guru-disciple relationship which exists *very commonly* in the Indian culture—would be available in the West, where there was no cultural basis for it. In the West, that kind of relationship wasn't familiar, it wasn't known, there were no models for it. The closest thing to it was a mentor relationship, which is not the Guru-disciple relationship.

So, he said that when he got this poem, and when he felt that connection which it revealed, his response was one of pleasure in seeing that *that* existed, and existed so profoundly. So yes, on the other side of the relationship there is a phenomenal experience. And there is pleasure involved in being connected to this Resonance as it is experienced by the disciple. It is pleasurable.

I don't remember the exact words you just used, but what you were referring to is this quality of connection that happens in the Presence between two body-mind mechanisms...and this is what you call Resonance?

Yes, there is a connection. There is a resonation between the two body-mind mechanisms. And that is unmistakable when it happens. My experience was that I went to Ramesh, and I was bowled over. Absolutely staggered by the experience of this Resonance that I found there. And it didn't really matter what he was speaking about. I mean, his teaching moved me, and that was nice, but there was something really deep and profound underneath all of the concepts. And that was what was important. That was what was potent. And so, I got on the phone to all my friends—both of them— *(laughs)* and I said, "You have to come and check this guy out! He's wonderful! I mean you go, you sit in his presence and you experience a window into the Infinite!"

They said, "Well, sure. Count us in. We'll go look through into the Infinite." They came along, and sat down, and listened and after it was over they looked at me and said, "Yeah, he's ah, nice. *(laughter)* Seems like a real nice guy, yeah. Really enjoyed what he had to say. You know I think he's probably really onto something." And it was clear that there was no connection. There was no Resonance there. Same Ramesh, different reactions.

I saw it happen countless times over the years. People would walk in and there was no Resonance. Many of them had come half way around the world to see him, with great anticipation, and they would sit down, and there was nothing there.

It's a pity.

It's what's happening.

There would be a lot more people.

Pardon me?

There would be a lot more people out there speaking, or living in a different way if they had had a connection with him.

Well, perhaps, yes. But so far, that has not been destined to happen.

Would you say that the disciple creates the medium?

The Guru-disciple relationship is a singular event. It is *an event.* And the notion that *one causes the other,* (one draws the other into being) is notional. I say it that way, only to point out that this quality of the body-mind mechanism that is generally thought of as the Guru, in and of itself, has no *Guruhood*; no more Guruhood than any other body-mind mechanism.

The notion is, that somehow when you get this Enlightenment, and thus get to be in the exalted position of "Guru," you have certain qualities, generally very exalted qualities! And as much as I would like to tell you that that is the case, I have difficulty doing so with a straight face and with my wife in the room. (laughter)

♋   ♋   ♋

RESONANCE WITH WAYNE

When I first came here I told you that I started with Alan Watts and others like him, and each one gave me pictures or plans and this and that. I was getting a general idea, but it's almost as if you came in like a professional architect and said "Here's a blueprint," and upon looking it over, I thought: "Ohmygod, ev-

erything fits in place!" That was my first impression of you, and what I continue to get now is this great feeling. I see an aliveness in your eyes that I didn't see in those other people, and I think that comes from the life-force and contact with it.

I would say that what you're experiencing *is* in fact the life-force, but it is your capacity to perceive it through this body-mind mechanism which creates the dynamic. There are lots of people who come here and have no such experience and contact nothing.

Really? I don't see how they could miss it.

Take my word for it. *(laughter)* Or take the word of lots of people who have brought their friends and co-horts to drink up what is here, yet whose friends went away thirsty. They go away without anything, looking at you slightly askance, saying: "Huh? What the hell is *wrong* with you?" Jeff and Susan brought half a god-damn meditation center to see me. *(laughter)* But none of them came back. I did the same thing with Ramesh. I brought several people to hear him speak, and they thought Ramesh was just fine...*for me* .

So, my attempt to describe this occurrence is how this term 'Resonance' came to be. I needed a term to describe that happening. I mean, there's no question that what I experienced with Ramesh was indeed there; yet, how was it that when *I* came and sat with him, there was this incredible connection, whereas when other people came, there wasn't? He certainly wasn't a different person with each of them, so, there was something that happened in the dynamic interaction between the two body-mind mechanisms that defined that experience. And the experience is unmistakable, it's not something that you've made up or that is some figment of your imag-ination. It's there, you know that it's there, and others who have experienced it will confirm that they experienced the same thing. They know that it is real. So, given that, this notion of Resonance came up, which in principle requires both the sage and the disciple to define that experience. Otherwise, the sage is just another body-mind mechanism through which Totality functions. He is no different from anyone else until the disciple with whom there is Resonance comes.

The Resonance is always on the part of the disciple. Now the relationship between the sage and the disciple will take on various characteristics depending upon the qualities of both the body-mind mechanism of the sage, and the body-mind mechanism of the disciple. Therefore, there can be what you could call personality clashes, in which they repel each other. Those are factors of having a personality. Just as when you walk into a room and look around, you say, "I like this person but that person is an idiot." You don't know either of those people, but you know that you like this person, and you know you don't like that person. And that has to do with who you are, and who they are. Call it chemistry if you will, call it vibes, juice, energy, whatever. All body-mind mechanisms have that with one another. And the body-mind mechanism of the sage is no different from any other body-mind mechanism. It is a hunk of meat that has various genetic properties. It has had various experiences, all of which combine to make it what it is in that moment, and determine how it responds in that moment.

The Resonance that you speak of isn't limited to the body-mind mechanism of the sage and of the devotee, is it?

No, in fact what makes the Resonance so unique is that it is not limited to the phenomenal...

But the phenomenal aspect is all we can talk about, right?

Yes, it is a part of it. Because what we are talking about is a phenomenal relationship. The relationship between the sage and the disciple is a relationship that exists within phenomenality. It exists between two body-mind mechanisms. Now, underlying that relationship is this quality that we're talking about. This magical, elusive quality that, once you've experienced it there is no denying that it exists. But trying to describe it to someone who has never experienced it is impossible. So, even after the so-called Awakening, there frequently is a continuation of the physical relationship between the sage and the disciple.

Is there any anticipation or excitement about seeing Ramesh, or do you always feel in contact? Is that just a ludicrous question?

Well it's not ludicrous. It's just that there isn't that kind of separation any more. I still very much enjoy being in his presence. It's a tremendously pleasurable experience for me, but I no longer feel like I 'need' it.

♋   ♋   ♋

RESONANCE WITH MARC AND MARGARETE

A couple of weeks ago you spent some time with Marc and Margarete, a couple of awakened souls. Is that a different experience from spending time with us?

Nope! *(laughter)* Not really. They're nice people, just like you are.

Do you see them as awakened?

There are no awakened individuals. I see those body-mind mechanisms just as I see any other body-mind mechanisms.

How do you see us?

As body-mind mechanisms. *(laughter)* I see you as characters on the stage playing out roles, just as this body-mind mechanism is on the stage playing out its role. All have characteristics, some of which I like, some of which I don't like. It is the nature of this organism, the preferences which are inherent in this organism, which determine all of that.

But you're not that body-mind mechanism?

No. None of us are. At the level we're talking about, we are all Consciousness. All there is, is Consciousness. We could not be anything other than Consciousness.

What you're saying is that Marc and Margarete are no different from us. You see them as no different from us?

Absolutely. They are characters in the Dream-Play. Each character has individual qualities. All of these characters have individual qualities. One of the qualities of those particular body-mind mechanisms is an absence of a sense of personal doership, which is a phenomenal quality, when it's associated with a body-mind mechanism.

Doesn't that absence though make one aware that one is just Consciousness?

It is, in fact, the absence of anyone to be aware of the fact that we are all just Consciousness. *(laughter)*

On the other side then, the lack of that absence is what creates all the anxiety.

The presence of that illusion creates suffering, just as the presence of the belief that a rope is a snake creates fear. The seeker asks, "How do I get away from the snake? How do I free myself from this fear of the snake?" The sage says, "There is no snake there," *(laughter)* and you say, "Okay, I believe you, but I'm still afraid of the snake."

But you could say the question is misconceived because it is the I Source that is asking it.

Yes, all of that is the same process. You walk in the room, you see it, and it appears to be a snake. The reaction that you have, if you are afraid of snakes, is fear! The image in your mind is that that is a snake. And when it is absolutely revealed to you that it is a rope, so that you see it as a rope when you walk in, there is no problem, you're not having to deal with the snake. There is neither the presence nor the absence of a snake to deal with.

I talked to a sage and something deep and profound happened. It was like I saw the Truth in everything. Now, that wouldn't have happened with just anyone, would it?

Probably not.

Why did that happen? How did that happen?

When there is Resonance between a seeker and a body-mind mechanism in which there is no sense of personal doership, there is that quality that you have described, in which there is an intuitive moment of seeing. It is very wonderful when that happens. What happens in that moment is your *absence*. It is a falling away of anyone to have any perceptions whatsoever. So, this quality of Truth or Oneness you experience is subsequent to it. It is applied when you come back.

When I come back?

When you come back, when that sense of 'youness' reappears...re-establishes itself, that is when there are all these qualities associated with an experience that you had. Then you say, "I had this experience, and it had these characteristics...there was Truth, there was this feeling of love. My heart opened. I experienced this, that or the other thing." Your background, and how you've been trained spiritually, will give the flavor to that experience of absolute nothingness. *That*, when it is brought into the phenomenal experience, has qualities. You give it qualities. You assign it qualities.

Why does the 'me' come back?

The time is not yet right for the Final Awakening in this particular body-mind mechanism to happen. Those experiences were what Ramesh calls, "free samples," or "glimpses over the fence."

$\cancer$ $\cancer$ $\cancer$

THE IMAGE OF THE SAGE

It's kind of a relief.

What's that?

I don't know why, it's just a relief. You just don't fit the persona, that's all. It's a relief. Everyone doesn't have to fit the persona.

I had that feeling when I met Ramesh. It was like, finally, *finally* there is a Master who is *ordinary*. It didn't make any sense to me that in order for there to be spirituality, you would have to deny all of your instincts, go live apart from everybody...what's that about?! That seemed to me to be the most artificial, bizarre kind of way to deny life. The message was that only the *spiritual* was real, and this life and living was all some kind of aberration. And you had to remove yourself from this life and cloister yourself away from it in order to find God! What's wrong with that picture? It never made any sense to me.

I had had the sense, long before I became a seeker, that religion was just bullshit. It was so patently ludicrous to me. And so, I just threw the whole thing out and said, "If that's what spirituality is, then screw it! Who needs it? A bunch of hypocrites, talking about, 'You must be pure. No sex.' And then they're fondling little boys in the back room. I mean, what kind of shit is that?" And of course, such things would happen, when you're trying to stuff down a very basic human quality. When you're trying to deny your essence, it's going to squish out sideways. So, all of that seemed ludicrous to me. Then I met Ramesh, and here was a guy who had been the president of a bank and was married, with three children. He had been educated at the *London School of Economics*, and had an incredible variety of experience in the world. Yet he was pointing to the fact that What Is, is God. What Is, is an expression of Consciousness, of the Totality. You don't have to deny this! Life isn't a screw up! You are not sinners. This isn't a sin. This is an expression of God. Even the horror. Even the so-called bad stuff, is all an expression of God, is *all* spiritual. I got that! That made sense to me. So, my reaction was similar to yours. *(sigh of relief)* Plus you save so much on robes and incense and mitres, and staffs. *(laughter)*

♈   ♈   ♈

NISARGADATTA MAHARAJ AND I AM THAT

I had a conversation with Ramesh about I Am That. Sathya Sai Baba had recommended it to some devotees, so I bought it and carried it back and forth to India hoping to read it some time, but I couldn't get past the first few chapters. Anyway, Ramesh said that there are people who don't like it because it seems to be contradictory. And no wonder—Ramesh described how what Maharaj said to one person might have been the exact opposite of what he would say to someone else.

Yes, and that's the case with any teacher who is worth his salt. He is going to be saying things to one person that are an absolute contradiction to what he says to somebody else, because what is happening is a response in the moment. It is the seeker who brings out the teaching from the Guru, not the other way around. Therefore, there are different seekers with, as Ramana Maharshi says, different levels of *dampness of gunpowder (laughter)*—certain seekers come to the Guru sodden, like sodden gunpowder, and you could hold a spiritual blowtorch to them and they are not going to ignite. *(laughter)* But others come tinder-dry, and the first word or just the sight of the Guru ignites them. Yet in both cases, the Guru isn't concerned at all.

I Am That is a great example of what happens to an initial notion. A lot of people believe that *I Am That* is Scripture—literally Scripture. They'll take pages and verses—they've got it memorized and underlined and circled, and they'll say, "This is what Maharaj said about this," and "This is what he said about that." He said, "You have to be earnest. You have to do this. The characteristic of Enlightenment looks like that," and it's all there in this *bible* in which the truth is set forth. Ramesh said: "You know, I hate to tell you this, but look at the process by which *I Am That* came about. You have a teacher who himself admittedly says, "I'm not a literate man. I can barely write. I talk about this subject which one can't talk about in the first place, using a fairly limited palate to paint the descriptions with." And he spoke in Marathi.

So then you have another fellow who comes along who is really moved by Maharaj and he is Polish—not a native Marathi speaker, nor a native English speaker—and he translates the Marathi into English. Now, he takes the concepts of this person who is saying, "These are just my limited concepts to describe that which can't be described," and he translates them using his understanding of what the concept is, in a language that isn't his native language, and he puts that into another language that isn't his native language—selecting, out of a large body of transcripts, those points which he, as the editor, feels are pertinent. That is how you then come up with a book that purports to be *The Truth of Maharaj*. Now, that whole process happened in phenomenality—there's no arguing that. And its effects have been incredibly profound for some, and mind-bogglingly limiting for others.

I read I Am That *a few times, and I like the beauty of the way the words and concepts were put together. I think that in each dialogue, each interchange, each person who spoke with Nisargadatta got something, and I felt that I got something that they got. I felt a physiological shift within myself as I read from chapter to chapter. I felt continually more rested. Didn't Nisargadatta say there was some special energy behind that book? Because one fellow said that he read it before he even met Nisargadatta and he became clear. He didn't even have to meet him, because he got it from the book and Nisargadatta said there was a spirit or some type of force working through that book.*

Well, of course, there is, but the same force is operating through an orange.

*I'm not arguing with what you're saying, because
there are different appeals to the mind, but if there is any
interest in that book, then obviously there is some effect
going on.*

Absolutely...for some. Others like me are completely unmoved.

But the book has value...

That book may, in a particular body-mind mechanism, have a very positive effect. I mean, those words
can produce a tremendous opening when they resonate,
and create a tremendous shift. Yet, others take those
words literally and create a world-view out of the concepts, and thus absolutely obliterate any presence or sense
of Being because everything is filtered through a conceptual haze that is created by reading and misinterpreting *I
Am That.*

*Or any book, for that matter: Ramana, or Papaji, or
Nisargadatta, or Ramesh.*

Any book.

The intellectualizing holds on that level.

Precisely.

*But I'm wondering if even so, there is a physiologi-
cal effect happening—if there is some benefit even while
the readers are holding it in their minds, whether some
subtle effect is happening to their bodies or nervous systems. Is the Master's Grace somehow working on them
behind the scenes, and that effect comes up to the surface
at some point?*

The Master's Grace is the Grace of Totality, and the Grace of Totality is working constantly—that's the only thing that is ever working. It isn't the Grace of the body-mind mechanism of Nisargadatta Maharaj or Ramesh, even though it appears to be. The Grace is flowing through those mechanisms, and when there's Resonance with a particular seeker, then the seeker says, "It is the Grace of my Guru Ramesh," or "It is the Grace of my Guru Nisargadatta Maharaj," or "It is the Grace of my Guru Ramana Maharshi." But it is the same Grace, if you will, flowing through all of them.

And yet the benefit of being in the physical presence of someone who knows who he is, what he is—just that physical presence often times is enough. There is something happening, because even though it may be temporary, it still has its value.

It can, but not necessarily. How many thousands of people would walk by Ramana Maharshi on the street and not bat an eyelash? To them he's just another little Indian guy in a diaper. *(laughter)* Nothing was felt, because there was no Resonance on the part of that body-mind mechanism with the body-mind mechanism of the sage.

If everybody woke up at once, it would be kind of boring.

Yes, so far, Totality seems to like the manifestation just as it is, otherwise it would be different. *(laughter)*

∽   ∽   ∽

ARE THERE DIFFERENCES BETWEEN GURUS?

So, is there a difference between Gurus? If you take the Guru's Guru as it were, Ramana Maharshi, whom everybody seems to think is supreme, one of the Great Gurus, would you say that that level of understanding which you have discovered, is the same, or does this deepen? Are there different levels of that understanding?

There is one Understanding. It is the same Understanding that expresses through the various Biggies. The ones that have gotten all the press—they get the big press usually after they're dead because this deification of the Guru requires distance, and death is the ultimate distance. When you are up close with the body-mind mechanism, it is revealed very quickly to be a *body-mind mechanism*, and it has characteristics, qualities, like any other body-mind mechanism, some of which you like, some of which are appealing, and others which are irritating. One of the great things that happened to me was, I got to spend a lot of time with Ramesh, personally, as his roadie. I was driving him around and setting up the equipment and we spent an enormous amount of time together. And what was revealed is that there was a body-mind mechanism there with a *personality*. Characteristics, quirks, qualities that were *not* Godlike! *(laughter)* And yet, that didn't diminish what I knew to be there. So, my definition of what the Guru was, expanded. It expanded beyond these very limited notions of the Guru as superman, as the embodiment of only the human characteristics that we admire.

♋   ♋   ♋

WHAT IS THE FUNCTION OF THE GURU?

If the Truth cannot be grasped or even spoken about, what is the jnani doing when he's trying to get you to catch the Truth with your intellect? Is he just getting you going in circles until your intellectual reasoning gives out?

He is not doing a goddamn *thing*. The talking that happens, happens as a result of the presence of a disciple. It is the presence of a disciple that brings forth the teaching. The true *jnani* has no need to do *anything*—certainly not talk about That which can't be talked about. The *jnani* knows that the force producing his utterances is utterly inescapable. That any word that issues forth through his lips could not be otherwise, just as their effects could not be otherwise, be they 'positive' or 'negative.' I put those words in quotation marks because the 'positive' or the 'negative' is from the standpoint of the individual and whatever yardstick is being used to measure them. You think of the *jnani* as being someone with an agenda and some objective like every other body-mind mechanism, but it is not so.

I guess in the apparent radical shift when you're switching from the phenomenality to the noumenality—would the body-mind ever say anything again if it wasn't motivated to, or is what is happening all just happening?

Well, what may motivate it to speak is if some thought arises, but it has no agenda for itself. Now, the body-mind mechanism is the instrument of Totality. There is no question of the body-mind mechanism doing anything of its own accord. It operates according to its nature, and its nature is its genetic coding combined with all of the subsequent environmental conditioning. Every body-mind mechanism does that regardless of its spiritual state.

So, what is the function of the sage?

The sage *Is*. The notion of functionality comes about when there is some objective. In order for something to be functional there has to be an objective. And if it's functional it advances that objective. It moves towards the goal. And the sage *Is*. The sage is a responsive mechanism, pure and simple. Whether, through the instrumentation of the sage, a particular disciple has some kind of understanding or not, is not at all part of the intention of the sage. The sage has no agenda, has no objective. The sage...

The teaching of the sage is the finger pointing to the moon.

Okay.

That's what you're doing here.

Thank you, I was wondering...(laughter)

That's what's happening here.

Ah-ha.

That is why all these bodies are here asking questions, and that's why the answers are coming.

That is precisely true. As part of the functioning of Totality, body-mind mechanisms show up here and ask questions. This body-mind mechanism responds accordingly. That's what is happening. What the outgrowth of all that is going to be...

...Nobody knows...

Nobody knows.

So, for you, all that was required of the Guru, was that he had this Understanding because it is the Under-

standing that you've got. You got the Understanding from him.

Well, I got the intellectual understanding pretty quickly. The teaching as I've outlined it here, is basically, with a few personal twists and turns, the same teaching that was imparted to me by Ramesh...conceptually, structurally. And it had some very positive effects on me personally. It made my life easier. There was a greater intellectual understanding, which created less personal involvement. As I would become involved in things, more and more often the thought would arise, "This is just the functioning of Totality! This is just what's happening. This Is!" Acceptance would come. And even when acceptance wouldn't come, there would sometimes be acceptance of the fact that I wasn't accepting. Which *is* acceptance! *(laughter)* That cuts off that horizontal involvement that is part of being a seeker. It even cuts off the voice that says, "I should be accepting, I'm a seeker, I *know* all the spiritual shit, why am I not accepting all of this? How could I be so STUPID? All I have to do is accept it, and I'd be at peace, and I'm not accepting it, what the hell is wrong with me?"

The realization that it is *all*—even the nonacceptance—part of the functioning of Totality, is acceptance, and with increasing frequency, for me, that would come.

So, what part of it would you need Ramesh for?

Ramesh was there. That relationship was as it was. It could not have been otherwise, I couldn't say I needed him or didn't need him. It was what it was. Another body-mind mechanism might not require the presence of a living Guru in order for there to be some kind of understanding, there are no rules. It's wonderful when you have one, it is the most fantastic of relationships. But the Ultimate Understanding—the shift from identification on the pendulum shaft to identification at the fulcrum can happen any time, anywhere, with or without preparation, with or without a human or non-human Guru. There is no prerequisite.

♋   ♋   ♋

HOW A GURU IS CREATED

Does Enlightenment happen to people—out of the blue—all over the place?

Yes, out of the blue. He may not have a spiritual context in which to put it, that describes it in a way that he would *(snaps fingers)* instantly say, "Oh yeah, well that was this Ultimate Understanding." One day a farmer just walks out of his field, and instead of turning towards home, he keeps going! Or, he doesn't. He walks out of his field, and goes home, and does the same thing as he has always done. He doesn't even talk to anybody about it, because there's nothing to talk about. Literally, there's *nothing there*, to talk about it. Or, it may be that he comes out of his field and goes home, and one of his neighbors says, "There's something different about you. What is it?" And he starts to talk. And that neighbor tells somebody else, "You should talk to Frank. It's incredible, what happened to him in the field the other day." *(laughter)* And so some other people come, and they tell a few people, and a writer comes. And he starts writing down what Frank says. And then he publishes a book, *Frank Says. (laughter)* And now people are coming from all over the world to hear Frank.

Now, I was *not* going to do this talking. I had no interest in being a teacher. None. This Understanding happened in 1989, I didn't tell anybody about it. I mentioned it to Ramesh, but it was no big deal, and I *certainly* wasn't interested in being a teacher. But one day these poems started coming. I was at my espresso bar down the street, where I went every day at three o'clock, and a poem came, so I borrowed a piece of paper and jotted it down. The next day, I brought my notebook and jotted a couple more down. And they kept coming, absolutely effortlessly. Every day a few more came, and at the end of a few weeks there were a hundred of them, and I sent them off to Ramesh, and he said, "These are good. You should publish them." I said "Okay." But I didn't *want*—as I said in my introduction—a bunch of miserable seekers cluttering up my living room, like they were at Ramesh's.

Every day he had a couple of people coming and sitting in his living room. That didn't appeal to me. I had a business, I had a family, what did I want with *that* scene? Plus, I'd been traveling around with him long enough to know that everything you say about this is just BULLSHIT. *Do I really want a job as a bullshit artist?*—I already had that. I was in business. So, I published the book, *No Way* under the pen name 'Ram Tzu' which is short for Ramesh and Lao Tzu (the two profound influences, the two voices that I respected most in the spiritual arena) and I let it go at that. And I went on blissfully unsagelike for quite a number of years. My business grew, my children grew, my life went on, and all was well. And then in 1996 my very successful exporting business disappeared overnight. I mean, disappeared. I was a middleman and I got unmiddled. *(laughter)* And in the unmiddling, I was out of business.

When July rolled around, and *Guru Purnima* came (for those of you who are like I was, and don't know all the buzz words, *Guru Purnima* is the holiday when one goes and visits one's Guru, to pay homage) I visited Ramesh. I had never before gone to see Ramesh on *Guru Purnima*. I often joked with him that I was the world's worst disciple since I never came. But for the first few years I was unaware that Guru Purnima existed and then my business duties didn't allow me to go. So this time, without a business, I was free to go to India. And while I was there, on Guru Purnima Day, I woke up in the morning, and jotted down another poem: *(reads much-thumbed handwritten sheet)*

Nearly
Nine years ago
Now
I wrote a poem
For a bespectacled
Banker from Bombay
Who touched me
Like no other…
Not wife, not child, not parent
Had before
Or ever would again.

With great
Good humor
He suffered
My flitting about him
And when at last
I immolated
In his divine flame
There was revealed
Pure Love unimaginable
The Ground of All Being.

In an endless moment
Of pure Grace
The Guru and disciple
The me and the other
Melted together
Into a liquid pool
From which…
Surprise!
Ram Tzu was born.

> How wondrous that
> The Divine Irony
> Remains
> In the bodies
> And psyches
> Of Ramesh
> And Wayne.
> The Love
> Is thus given form
> And substance
> In this dream
> So bitter
> So sweet
> In this world where God
> Writes poems to Himself.

I gave Ramesh this poem in the morning, and he was quite moved and he asked me to read it for the group at the Guru Purnima talk—in fact he sent the servant out to have it Xeroxed and handed copies out to all who attended. I read the poem, and at the end of the talk he said, "You should all come back tomorrow—tomorrow Wayne's giving the talk."

I imagined since I wasn't Indian and I didn't have any spiritual trappings, nobody was going to come to listen to me! I figured I was safe. But the next day, some people came, and so I gave the talk. Or more precisely I gave about half the talk because Ramesh is a bit like a racehorse. You take a racehorse out onto the track, and he's going to run. You can't tell him, "This isn't your race." *(laughter)* So, about half way through the talk there was a lull, and in the lull Ramesh kind of looked around and saw that there was a lull and that seemed intolerable to him so off he went. *(laughter)* Which was absolutely fine with me.

A couple of weeks later somebody called from Atlanta and said, "We hear you're talking. We have a small group here and we'd really appreciate it if you'd come

out and talk with us. I said, "Well, okay." And I went.
Then somebody else called. And the phone has kept ringing. People keep showing up, and a few even come back.
Much to my surprise this talking, which seemed that I
was absolutely temperamentally unsuited for, happens.
I would sit with Ramesh in his talks, talk after talk and
listen to him tell the same stories time after time. He told
the same jokes, and there were the same people in different bodies *(laughter)* city after city, asking the same
questions, giving the same responses. And I thought, "I
could never do this in a million years. I don't have this
kind of patience." Well, incredibly when the seeker comes
and there's Resonance, the teaching happens. And it
doesn't have much to do with Wayne or his personality,
and it doesn't have much to do with the personality in
the seeker who comes. But in that alchemy that happens
between the two body-mind mechanisms, the teaching
arises. And whether it arises in words or it arises in silence, there it is.

So, a year passed between Guru Purnimas, 1996 and
1997. In that year a lot of talking went on. I started to
travel around and meet a lot of people. And the following Guru Purnima I went to Bombay again. And I brought
with me some tapes that had been made at my talk in
Sedona. On Guru Purnima of that year no poem came,
but I wrote Ramesh a note, and I attached it to these tapes.
I gave it to him on the morning of Guru Purnima...

July 20, 1997
Dear Ramesh,

On this Guru Purnima I give to you this set of tapes
from my recent series of talks in Sedona. I do this without the slightest expectation that you'll ever listen to
them. I haven't listened to them either. I present them to

you as a symbol of how the teaching is moving onward. Of how the Grace of the Guru is transmitted in seemingly the most unlikely of ways by some of the most unlikely of characters. And of what chaos you have wrought by unleashing me on this unsuspecting world.

You tell me you're unsurprised by all of this, and I do believe you. To me it remains an ongoing source of amazement. Though since that fateful day in the LA airport when your words unveiled my future as your publisher, I have suspected that you can see far more about me than can I. You have embraced me as a son, brought me into your home, and given me the gift that surpasses all understanding. And there is not enough gold or enough words to express my gratitude. I must remain content with the knowledge that you too know the bhaktic ecstasy of being consumed by the Guru. And thus realize that these words, though *inescapable*, are inadequate and ultimately superfluous. The Guru and disciple are One. It has *always* been so. It forever will be so. This, according to my dear Ramesh, is the Final Truth.

♋   ♋   ♋

So this is what I do now. People come and we talk about that which can't be talked about. Sometimes we sit in the Silence together. Sometimes we laugh and sometimes we cry. When there is this Resonance, the mind and no-mind are revealed to be equally Divine, and there is a profound acceptance of What Is.

I will leave you now with a few words I wrote while sitting with Ramesh in Germany during our seminar there in 1999. It is such a blessing to know this Love of and for the Guru. If you have yet to drink from this deepest of all wells...I wish it for you Now.

♋   ♋   ♋

So
What's the deal?

Sitting with a toothless old man
Beside a fire
The house silent
Before the rain.
He sits eyes closed
Frail
Skin and bones
Encased in pajamas
And a sweater
Barely there.

Why do my eyes fill with tears?
Why does my heart swell
Threatening to break free of my chest?
After so many years with him
You'd think I'd be used to it.

His eyes flick open
And catch me watching him
They are the eyes of
A bird of prey
Piercing
Relentless
Eyes that see small details
From a great distance
Pitiless
Compassionate
The eyes of my Master
The eyes of a Sage.

Empty handed I entered the world.
Barefoot I leave it.
My coming, my going -
Two simple happenings
That got entangled.

Kozan Ichikyo, Death Poem
1583-1660.

INDEX

More From Advaita Press

A Duet of One by Ramesh S. Balsekar

Here Ramesh uses the Ashtavakra Gita as a vehicle for an illuminating look at the nature of duality and dualism. Softcover 224 Pages $16.00

Who Cares?! by Ramesh S. Balsekar

This is the boook we recommend to those asking for a book that will describe the essence of Ramesh's teaching. Ramesh's ability to cut through to the simple heart of complex ideas is a joy to experience. Softcover 220 Pages $16.00

The Final Truth by Ramesh S. Balsekar

The Final Truth is one of the most complex and rewarding of Ramesh's written works. It may well be the most comprehensive look at Advaita currently in print. It takes us on a rich and vivid journey from the arising of "I AM" to the final dissolution into identification as pure Consciousness. Softcover 240 Pages $16.00

Your Head In The Tiger's Mouth by Ramesh S. Balsekar

A superb overview of the Teaching. Transcribed portions of talks Ramesh gave in his home in Bombay during 1996 and 1997.
Softcover 472 Pages $24.00

A Net Of Jewels by Ramesh S. Balsekar

A handsome gift volume of jewels of Advaita, selections from Ramesh's writings presented in the format of twice daily meditations. Hardcover 384 Pages $25.00

Consciousness Speaks by Ramesh S. Balsekar

Ramesh's most accessible and easy to understand book. Recommended both for the newcomer to Advaita and the more knowledgeable student of the subject. Softcover 392 Pages $19.00

Ripples by Ramesh S. Balsekar

A brief and concise introduction to Ramesh's Teaching. Perfect to give to friends. Softcover 44 Pages $6.00

SEE NEXT PAGE FOR ORDERING DETAILS

www.advaita.org

NO WAY *for the spiritually advanced* by Ram Tzu

 No Way is a unique blending of wit, satire and profound spiritual insight. One minute we are howling with unconstrained laughter, the next we are squirming in self-conscious recognition as Ram Tzu holds up a perfect mirror and then gleefully points out that we aren't wearing any clothes.
Softcover - 112 Pages $13.00
Also available on Audio Cassette $15.00

===============